THE PRACTICE OF ASTROLOGY

*As a Technique in Human
Understanding*

by

DANE RUDHYAR

1978
SHAMBHALA
BOULDER & LONDON

Shambhala Publications, Inc.
1920 13th Street
Boulder, Colorado 80302

*This work is dedicated to
Margaret E. Hone
in appreciation of the openness
and integrity of her spirit.*

TABLE OF CONTENTS

INTRODUCTION

The text-books on astrology which have been written during the last seventy-five years reveal a definite evolution in astrological thinking and even in the character of astrological techniques. During the nineteenth century, English astrologers were in the forefront of the movement toward a re-statement and popularization of this ancient system of thought, but they followed strictly in the footsteps of their Medieval and Renaissance predecessors, who in turn did little more than repeat what had been said by Ptolemy during the great days of the Roman Empire, when a vast era of human development was closing which had seen the birth, spread and triumph of astrology. Today, however, four basic trends are definitely manifest in astrology.

The first trend is a popularization of the simplest elements in astrology, those referring to the position of the Sun and the planets in the Zodiac, and to their "transits" over the important points in the natal chart. This trend seeks to blend in varied proportions the fundamental methods of ancient and Medieval astrology with the broad psychological knowledge which has been spread throughout the United States.

The second trend is shown in an attempt to establish astrological findings upon a statistical and empirical basis which would give them a more "scientific" character and which might insure the eventual recognition of astrology by academic thinkers.

The third trend, appearing only here and there, is the result of a desire to correlate astrology with new or revised "esoteric" doctrines along the lines of occultism, Oriental or Occidental.

The fourth trend originates in the frank recognition of the symbolical character of astrology as a technique for a basic understanding of Nature, and, above all, of human nature. Astrology, accord-

7

ing to such an approach (which is the one taken by this writer), is shown to have been essentially, from the very dawn of human civilization, *the result of man's attempt to understand the apparent confusion and chaos of his life-experiences by referring them to the ordered patterns of cyclic activity which he discovers in the sky.*

Astrology is born of the poignant need in every man for order. Celestial phenomena reveal such an order; and using this order as a measuring stick and clock, man, by referring all that happens within and around him to it, satisfies at last his yearning for harmony. He learns to identify his consciousness and will with the "celestial" patterns and rhythms. He becomes one with the principle of universal order, which many call "God". And living an ordered life he becomes an integrated person: a man of wisdom. Though the energies of his own nature or of society at war may beat upon his consciousness through the gates of his senses and his feelings, yet he himself, as a centralized and integrated Self, is at peace. For, to him, even the most destructive storm has its place and function within the order of his destiny, or of mankind's destiny. And by "destiny" he means: the complete whole of a cycle of living.

Astrology, in such a conception of its character and use, is a technique for the gaining of wisdom through the understanding of the order in human nature and in all phenomena perceived by man: *a technique in understanding.*

Astrology as a technique in human understanding: this is, I believe, the deepest and most vital characterization I can establish of this system of thought which has been so greatly abused and so greatly misused. However, there is no attempt on my part to belittle the possibilities of forecasting the future which astrology undoubtedly offers to the master in this difficult art; and indeed no one acquainted with "horary astrology" can ever deny its amazing potentialities. But in order to use constructively and wisely these potentialities the astrologer need have gained more than mere technical proficiency - difficult even as such a gain is. He must also

have reached a high degree of human understanding. For what the
sky reveals is nothing but *raw materials for human understanding.*
Everything ultimately depends upon individual understanding.
This is so in astrology, as it is in medical or psychological therapy.
Knowledge, in these fields, is not enough. Wisdom is needed.

The usual astrological text-books, old and new, are filled with
data, the memorizing of which insures knowledge. But wisdom is
an elusive factor. It can hardly be taught. It may partly be transferred from living person to living person. Yet, because it is based
on the full understanding of total situations and of experiences
lived without any reservations, it can only be acquired through
actual living, through pain, through the discharge of responsibilities, through the courageous and honest putting forth of the whole
of oneself in whatever experience is seen as significant.

Nevertheless, knowledge can be geared to the attainment of wisdom. And in this work, my aim is to make a presentation of the
basic concepts and facts used in modern astrology which is as
simple and clear as possible without losing sight of the ultimate
goal of this kind of astrology: the development of human understanding. Each chapter of this book is thus conceived as outlining
a basic step toward astrological wisdom. If the reader is not yet
acquainted with the ordinary methods used in astrology, what is
written should provide him with a sound basis for further and more
detailed study. If the reader is thoroughly familiar with astrological techniques, I trust that he will find here a challenge to further thinking and the stimulation to seek always for deeper human
values while using the astrological tools.

THE FIRST STEP

To Understand the Nature and Purpose of what One is about to Study

One may acquire knowledge without enquiring into the nature of the subject one is about to study, or into the purpose of the study; but wisdom will ever elude the man who is contented with accumulating facts and technical data. Wisdom is based on *useable knowledge* - and on the purposeful use of it. Therefore the aimless approach to astrology, or the approach based on mere personal curiosity, should be transformed by a clear recognition of the nature and goal of astrology, if the study of astrology is to orient man toward a deeper understanding of human nature and of all manifestations of life. Every student - however casual his study - should ask honestly to himself: what does astrology mean to me? What is my aim in becoming better acquainted with it?

No one can answer these question for the student, but the considerations which follow should help to make him more aware of the nature and the limitations of astrological thinking and astrological practice.

Astrology and Astronomy

Astronomy is the scientific study of celestial phenomena. It studies *how* things happen in what we call the universe.

Astrology, on the other hand, is a technique of symbolization and of prognostication, in which some selected categories of astronomical data are used as *indicators* of the behaviour of the basic functional activities within "organic wholes" and of the structural characteristics displayed by these wholes. Astrology does not attempt to tell in a scientific manner how things happen, either in the sky or in human beings. Astrology does not describe phenomena or events; nor does it seek to grasp the chain of causes and effects in any of the matters it touches. Astrology, as I understand it, has no concern whatsoever with whether a conjunction of planets *causes* some things to happen to a person or a nation; it only *indicates* the possibility or probability of a certain type of events occurring in a certain place at a certain time. It does not tell us why or how the event occurs, no more than a clock striking noon tells us why or how the sensation of hunger arises in the consciousness of the worker accustomed to eat at such a time of the day-cycle. The conjunction and the sound of the clock merely point to the normal expectancy of a certain type of condition taking place at a particular time in a man's consciousness.

Astrology is primarily a method for the interpretation, at several levels, of the *relationship between causally unrelated sets of phenomena.* This simply means that astrology "interprets" the observable concurrence between celestial phenomena and more or less definite changes in the lives of individuals or groups, but it is not concerned with the scientific study of the cause of such a concurrence, except on a purely philosophical or metaphysical basis. Such a scientific study could be attempted and some astrologers are making such an attempt on rather slim foundations; but the success or failure of the attempt does not affect the astrological findings and does not add any significant value to astrology as a "technique in human understanding". Astrology is a study of an observable parallelism between the *timing of events* in the universe and in the individual consciousness. It is a study of time-pieces; for every planet, and the Sun and Moon, are in astrology time-pieces which enable us to find the state of development in time (the point of maturity) of the various organic activities and functions within all living organisms.

Definition of "Organism" and "Organic Whole"

An organism is an organized living being which is born, comes to maturity and dies, or becomes transformed into some other form of life. A cell, a plant, an animal, and a human being are organisms. Beside such actually living entities, there are what we shall call "organic wholes". These are systems of mutually related elements and activities constantly interacting, and having some kind of more or less permanent identity. A nation, a business corporation, and even a particular well- defined situation caused by the coming together of several individuals who remain closely interrelated, constitute "organic wholes". These also can be said to be born, to develop and mature, then to disintegrate according to a measurable rhythm. They have a recognizable basic *structure*.

The term "structure" is considered here in its broadest meaning, and it can be modified by special uses in relation to special sets of factors. Structure does not refer only to the particular organization of physical materials - as when we speak of the skeleton as the basis of the body-structure. We can speak also of the structure of an electro-magnetic field: that is, of the web of "lines of force", which are made visible only when iron-fillings are placed in that field. I will be mentioning often the structure of the psyche, of the mind; the structure of functions, at one level or another.

What is meant by structure is always the more or less permanent results of the workings of a principle of organization. It refers to the web of relationships within the limits of the organic whole; to the *place* occupied by the various organs within this whole, to the *schedule* of their joint operations: structure in space - structure in time. The former, structure in space, is Form; the latter, structure in time, Rhythm. The full and perfect Form is the Sphere; the complete Rhythm manifests as the Cycle.

As we use the term function here, it characterizes activities which play a well-defined, regular and recurrent part in the life of an organism, whether at the physiological or psychological level. The activities of the organs and cells of the body are all related to the entire behaviour of the organism as a whole, and they are interacting and interdependent. Likewise the activities which come under the categories of thinking, feeling, willing, etc. are also to be considered as "functional" for they should always be referred to the whole personality and studied in their mutual relationships.

The fuctions of the body have acquired throughout the ages of human evolution a remarkable stability and their interdependence is so well organized that all kinds of automatic mechanisms preserve constantly the health (i.e. the integration) of the organism. These mechanisms of self-restoring wholeness and health are not yet adequately developed at the psychomental levels of human activity. Thus the problem of personal-psychological integration is often acute, even where the person is supposedly sane and successful. This is particularly so today in a time of social, political and world-wide upheavals.

What is the Main Subject-Matter of Astrology?

It is the individual human person considered as an integral organism including bodily, psychic, mental, social and spiritual activities of many types and at several levels. The terms body, mind, feelings, soul define loosely these various types or categories of activities. All these activities are "human" activities because, however similar some of these may be to the activities displayed in other kingdoms of life (animal, vegetable, etc.), they are nevertheless polarized by, and essentially subservient to, a generic pattern and purpose which is characteristic of the human kingdom and exclusive to it. Man may digest his food like other mammals, but in as much as he can be conscious of this digestive process and can interfere with it deliberately - for good or ill - digestion in all men is "human".

The field of astrological interpretation extends to any relatively permanent group of human persons or to any situation within the flux of human experience. Groups or series of natural phenomena - as for instance those referring to the weather - can also be analyzed and their development interpreted by means of astrological

13

charts, but, essentially, only in so far as they are parts of the collective experience of human beings.

The basic purpose of astrology is to bring order to the apparent chaos of man's experience, and thus help the individual or the group to achieve a greater degree of integration, health and sanity. It is to build a more conscious approach to human life and a deeper understanding of the structural characteristics and of the cyclic behaviour of all organisms. Thus its importance; for it is man's prerogative and spiritual obligation to tread the "conscious Way".

However, astrology offers no shortcut to integration, because the integration of any organic whole is a gradual process depending, on one hand, upon the very intensity of the feeling of "order", and of the realization of "center", in the many parts of this whole - and on the other hand, upon the readiness of the spiritual Principle linked with this organism-in-the-making to dynamize and illumine the organism's efforts toward complete and harmonic organization. Moreover, every factor which is to be seen in an astrological chart can contribute either to personal integration or to disintegration. What the birth-chart does is to present in a special manner the data which the psychologist and the physician use in their therapies.

The manner of this presentation, however, throws an entirely new light upon the component parts, functions, drives and potentialities of the individual personality. By the use of this new light, a person who understands well its value and the way of handling it is able to become more fully objective to himself. He is able to chart the course of his organic development, to plot the curve of his life-powers, and *to see himself reduced to essentials*. Underneath the confusion of his everyday experience, he comes to discern a pattern of order. All his conflicting tendencies reveal themselves as complementary components of his integral personality. He sees himself whole, in structure and function.

What he sees, however, is *not* a graphic image or portrait. He sees only a symbol. The birth-chart is only a symbol: the "name" of the total person. But by learning to spell this "name", the individual may find - if he be wise! - how best to strive, in his own way, toward actual and everyday-demonstrated integration. The astrologer-psychologist can only point the way to him. The individual alone can utter the "name", symbol of integral selfhood. He utters it only by living significantly and fully what he is, within the larger framework of society and humanity.

Predictability is a consequence of ordered development. If there is complete order in the universe, then one may be able to predict what next phase of a cycle will follow the present phase. If predictability were an illusion there could be no science, no generalization and no law. In so far as astrology is a science it must therefore include predictions.

Astronomy is a system of prediction of celestial phenomena. Astrology, however, does not deal with the determination of celestial phenomena, but with their *interpretation* in terms of human character and behavior. When a planet is given a certain meaning in astrology, this meaning is conditioned, both, by its astronomical features within the solar system, and by what it represents in relation to the total human person (or total situation affecting the individual). Any one of the planetary meanings presupposes the existence of *complete persons* as the frame of reference for such meanings. Astrology refers thus always, implicitly to the totality of human nature, as expressed in an individual.

Obviously, therefore, no astrological meaning or judgment is ever fully expressed which does not take in consideration the whole human being. To say that two planets will be conjunct at a certain time is astronomical. To add that the life of a man born at a certain time and place will experience a crisis, the date of which can be ascertained - is an astrological statement. In this statement the starting point is "the life of a man". Any prediction which does not take this whole entity "the life of a man" as a foundation or frame of reference is at best incomplete. It is, in most cases, misleading; in some cases, actually destructive. It has value only as it is shown in its relation to the whole individual person, *and to what it contributes to this person's development,* at one level or another.

15

Astrology does not predict "events" but only phases in a person's development. Every individual person develops along lines which are first of all "generic" - that is, which results from the simple fact that he is a *human* being, member of the genus, *homo sapiens,* at a particular time of mankind's evolution. These lines of development determine the general pattern of the life-span of every man. Likewise every man has basic bio-psychological characteristics which determine his *generic structure*. On this theme, human nature, races and individuals produce variations of many kinds. A man is first human, then white-skinned, then American, than a Californian of English-French ancestry, then a Methodist, a Democrat, etc. - and lastly he is an individual born at a certain time and on a particular spot.

Free will is the measure of a man's capacity to be and act as an individual. Fate is the measure of his dependence upon collective and generic standards as determining structures.

Astrology deals first with human nature in a generic sense; as it does so, it can be fairly certain that the known order of normal phases of human development will be approximately experienced by the client in as much as he is a human being; and this gives the astrologer a basis for prediction. Yet no astrologer should stop there. He should seek to define and understand the "individual equation" in his client - which means, the way the client does, and can be expected to react to the basic turning points of his life *as an individual*. This can only be done by considering the birth-chart and its time-development *as a whole*. The individual is the whole-man, the integral person. And no one can determine in advance the actions and reactions of an integral person who has become truly individualized; for such a person has become free, within the limits of his generic structures. Astrology can define the limits, but it can only suggest the freedom. Every moment of the life of an individual is a composite of both these factors.

16

THE SECOND STEP

To Assume Personal Responsibility for the Use of One's Knowledge

Wisdom is useable and purposeful knowledge put to work in everyday living. There is a type of knowledge which, as it mainly offers a mass of unrelated data to be memorized, clutters up the individual's path toward wisdom. But there is another type of knowledge which is geared to a vital desire for wisdom, and which leads to an eventual realization of the wholeness and integrity of the individual person. This last type of knowledge is based on principles of order which are universally valid; their application illumines all matters being studied. It is knowledge which appeals to the individual thinker within every man, woman and child; which summons this thinker out of his sleep and laziness; which, once used regularly, makes a man a *power* in the universe: A power for good, if the individual sees himself as a conscious participant in the activities of a greater whole - be it called society, humanity, or God; a power for destruction, if the individual seeks only self-aggrandizement and finds no value in anything except his rugged individualism and isolationism.

What I am seeking to present in this book is a graded, step-by-step approach to the study of astrology which leads to clear thinking and to the type of knowledge enabling the individual not only to live in the way of wisdom and psychological integration, but also to share constructively this knowledge with others. The first step in any valid course of study is quite obviously "to understand the nature and purpose of what one is about to study" - and the

17

preceding chapter has been devoted to that step. What follows - the second step in the acquisition of astrological wisdom - has not only a less obvious character, it actually is left in the distant background of the mind by most people who seek after knowledge, and knowledge only.

A thorough consideration of this second step would actually lead us to a critical analysis of the very foundation of our modern civilization. This is naturally beyond the scope of this present study, yet a few basic points must be stated which are susceptible of general application in all fields of knowledge.

Knowledge Leads to Responsibility

We live in a period of civilization which has been characterized not only by a tremendous increase in human knowledge, but also by the inability displayed by the leaders of mankind to assume any responsibility whatsoever for that knowledge. Ways and means to control powerful natural energies have been devised by man during the last centuries and they have been made known to whomsoever had the intellectual capacity to memorize certain types of data and to follow attentively given recipes for the application of this public scientific knowledge. But the scientist and the inventor of techniques and machines feel in no way responsible for the use to which the knowledge they disseminate will be put. Nor do the leaders of the state assume any responsibility for what the people they guide or rule do with what is placed in the public's hands!

Modern man is a person who uses indiscriminately the products of a knowledge of which he has no vital and *human* understanding, and the fundamental purpose and ultimate value of which he does not even question. Modern man is interested in technique first and last. *How to* use the tools of knowledge after an easy course of training; how to get quick results in terms of effective operation and application - this is all that counts for him. A man buys a car and drives it. He does not understand the nature of the energies and of the mechanical processes which make the car operate. He does not comprehend the relation of this car and its power to the universe, nor does he contemplate the relation of his driving it to society's welfare or even to his own ultimate good. He uses the products of human knowledge and skill, but he assumes no responsibility for that use, beside what the law says he must do in case he hurts somebody; and even that responsibility is shifted to an insurance company gambling with death.

The astrologer often acts in a somewhat similar manner. He learns a technique. He learns how to read his tables, and how to interpret the symbols of his craft. With practice and attention, with some degree of innate perspicacity, and with not a little good luck, he may succeed in applying astrological rules and in using the intellectual tools at his disposal in an effective manner. He may predict ahead of time the death of a President, the outcome of a famous lawsuit or the occurrence of an earthquake; and if he does he is considered a "success" - nay more, a "great astrologer". People flock to him, asking for personal advice, throwing their hectic lives at him in eager anticipation for predictions, for good news, for anything to break the monotony and spiritual emptiness of most modern lives. Colloquially speaking, the astrologer "knows his stuff" - and he "dishes it out". He gives information, as he sees it in the charts. More information, as the client returns. Always more data, more knowledge. It may be real knowledge; the facts are there and he reads them correctly. One problem, however, may not enter his mind as he goes through the scheduled time allotted for the interview: What use will the client make of the information? The client has been given a 12-cylinder car; but perhaps he has only a 4-cylinder mind to handle it. The information was correct. Was the imparting of it *wise?*

I defined wisdom as "useable and purposeful knowledge put to work in everyday living". I could have added that it is knowledge for which we assume personal responsibility. We assume personal responsibility for it the moment we refuse to separate knowledge in itself from the purpose of knowledge in terms of *human* values. To impart knowledge without caring to discover whether or not this knowledge is *assimilatable* by those to whom it is given, and

whether - once assimilated - it will have a sporting chance to be
conducive to personal or group integration is to fail to assume
responsibility for that knowledge. It is to follow the way of the
intellect, not the path of wisdom. It is to divorce analytical thinking from integral living, intellectuality from moral values, the brain
from the heart.

Our modern civilization and its total, devastating wars are the
outcome of such a divorce. Science has run foul of humanity. It is
said that knowledge is power; but power of itself has no meaning
- just as speed of itself has no meaning. Power for what? Speed
to reach what? Power becomes "human" only when its use and
its purpose are consciously evaluated, and the responsibility for the
results is assumed in clear understanding. This does not mean that
the results deliberately sought need be constructive. There will always be individuals who will seek knowledge for ends which are
destructive of the lives or possessions of others. But in such cases
the issue is clear, as in a struggle between viruses and antibodies -
and the will to health and sanity in most cases wins. What is dead-
ly is the confusion which comes from the irresponsible and vaguely
well-meant use of knowledge, from the handling of tools and techniques by minds without moral maturity, without the basic understanding of human nature and of the cyclic development of that
nature, without being aware of the fateful results which an information given carelessly, imprecisely or incompletely, and out of
time can cause.

I am concerned essentially here with the practice of astrology,
whether it be self-practice or practice directed to the solution of
other persons' problems. friends as well professional clients; but
obviously, what I am stating applies in general as well to psychologists, psychiatrists, doctors - and also educators, community leaders or statesmen. A doctor, before receiving his degree, must take
the Hippocratic oath. He is committed by tradition, by law, and
by moral pressure to use his knowledge beneficiently and in a spirit
of self-sacrifice. Yet many are the physicians who fail to understand that the information they give to their patients has value on-

ly according to the patient's ability to face it constructively and assimilate it. They fail to realize what every psychiatrist and "spiritual guide" should realize, but often does not: viz. that the official possession of knowledge gives them *authority*. To have authority is more than to have knowledge. It is to be *accepted* as a man with knowledge - perhaps with wisdom. And this means a profound increase of responsibility.

Authority and Astrological Practice

The psychologist who has his official Ph. D. degree, or who has written widely praised books, has authority as a result of this more or less official recognition. As a result the patient who comes to him is ready to accept his diagnosis and his technical procedures as valid. In the astrologer's case there is no official guarantee of astrological skill available; on the contrary, official standards of value are all against astrology. The practice of astrology may even be against the law of state or city. Yet, the astrologer has authority as one who deals understandingly and effectively with the mysterious and the incomprehensible, or the occult.

There is a part of every man's mind that is dissatisfied with things as they officially are, with the knowledge available to everyone. The search for a knowledge of realities and of energies beyond the known may be called escapism; yet it is also the deepest trait of human nature. "Threshold knowledge" - and all occultism is such a knowledge - has a fascination for man, probably because, as I once wrote, the "greatness of man is that he can always be greater". But in order to reach the "greater", man must step over a threshold. And in order to do that he must be guided - guided by someone who presents himself with the attributes of authority. Astrology is threshold knowledge. He who is able to use such a knowledge possesses the authority of the as-yet-incomprehensible. And this authority imposes upon the astrologer a heavy personal responsibility, whether or not he admits it, whether or not he cares to act accordingly.

Astrology deals with symbols - or some may say with transcen-

21

dent and cosmic forces. The psychotherapist, since Freud and Jung, works also with elements which appear quite transcendental and mysterious - with "dreams", with psychic "images" or "complexes". Yet the dreams are, after all, the client's own. But when the astrologer speaks of Mars, Jupiter, Saturn, he deals with entities which are eminently mysterious and whose effective actions are beyond the pale of normal scrutiny. Thus, the person who becomes an astrologer's client must have faith, or at least the queer borderland feeling in which curiosity, skepticism and an avid eagerness to believe blend. As the astrologer talks of these remote entities, the planets, the ordinary client senses the power of mysterious Forces operating in his life. He is led to the realm of a "threshold knowledge"; he is led, in most cases, blindfolded and without any bearings. Yet he who leads him and pours into his mind and psyche starting information has, in most cases, very little sense of responsibility *for what this information evokes in the client's consciousness.*

All knowledge engenders responsibility for him who shares or else who refuses to share it for fear of responsibility! But the imparting of "threshold knowledge", with its potent symbols and mysterious entities or forces, produces far more responsibility, for he who receives the knowledge must accept it on authority and on faith - as a young child is taught by his parents.

Astrology and Fear

The personal responsibility of the astrologer to his clients, his friends or hearers reveals itself conclusively as one deals with the source of practically all negative psychological factors: fear. Fear is born of lack of understanding, but even more of a feeling of inadequacy. One fears any confrontation to the facing of which one feels unequal, or for which one believes oneself (rightly or wrongly) to be unprepared. Man is constantly faced by the possibility of becoming greater than he is; and most of the time he shrinks from taking the steps ahead, because he lacks self-confidence and feels inferior to the task or the opportunity - or because he is too attached to his last success and his established happiness. In either case, fear manifests. For, if a man refuses to move ahead because he is happy where he is, it is essentially that he fears the loss of his present happiness or his inability to gain anything as satisfactory.

Yet man senses at certain times the need for change - even in areas in which he rebels most desperately against change. First, the imminence of a crisis disturbs him; then, the actual pressure of the growing life within begins to shatter his old psychological, mental or physiological structures, his beliefs and his habits - and he becomes frightened. It is then that a man or woman seeks a psychologist, a spiritual guide, or an astrologer. In some cases, there is no immediate or individually conscious sense of crisis or fear, yet all humanity is caught in a condition of collective crisis. It is because of this that men are seeking more than ever to comprehend any type of "threshold knowledge", occultism, astrology - anything which might lead to a really new sense of living, a new understanding. Yet what they bring to these types of knowledge is, above all, their fear; then, their need for personal guidance.

Does the ordinary astrologer recognize this fact? Not clearly, if at all. He sees the obvious: the man's and woman's curiosity, their yearning to hear someone talk about themselves, the desire to know "what is going to happen". But all these things are masks over the dim countenance of fear. Change is impending; change has come; change is ploughing deep the contented soil of yesterdays. Change is pain. Men question the stars because they are in chaos, in darkness, in a bewildering fog. Astrology must answer for men the question of the existence of order. The known order of the earth and of human society is shattered. Souls that are dark and anguished turn to the stars - others turn to God and His supposed representatives among men.

This is not making an unnecessarily dark picture. It is dealing with psychological facts. The persons who come with serious intent to an astrologer for advice are people who are insecure, thus potentially afraid. They want the security which a new knowledge might give them, and they want guidance. The astrologer who answers their questions fails them essentially if he or she is unprepared or unwilling to assume personal responsibility for the information and the advice given. He fails them tragically if, instead of helping the client to overcome his semi-conscious fears, he accentuates and gives a mysterious power to these fears by giving them a justification against which there can be no recourse. "Saturn is squaring your Sun. Watch out!" The person came disturbed, confused and sensing difficulties ahead; he leaves the astrologer's office with a crystallized expectation of tragedy. "Saturn" is about to hurt him; his wife *may* die, or his kidney *may* need an operation. Saturn. What is there one can do about Saturn, or to Saturn? Nothing apparently. Fear has taken shape and name. The anticipation of disaster torments the mind. It is worse still for being only half-known, elusive, mysterious. Every worried look in the wife may be the beginning of her end; every pain in the back may herald the unopposable advance of the dark Power, Saturn, remote in the unreachable sky.

It will not help the situation to say the "influence" of Saturn is of the nature of electro-magnetic waves; or that it can be expressed in a statistical average. It may be much worse to know one's husband has 75% chances of dying or becoming insane, than to know he *will* die or become insane. Uncertainty breeds devastating fear far more than the confrontation with the inevitable. And let us not say "forewarned, forearmed!" It does *not* apply where Mars, Saturn, squares, oppositions are presented as objective, *evil entities* which are actually and concretely doing something to men. It does not apply where there is fear. The astrologer's client is told he may meet with an accident affecting his head on Sunday. Cautiously he stays in bed - and the cord supporting a heavy painting on the wall alongside of which his couch rests breaks; he is badly hurt. Or else he walks in the street looking everywhere for a brick to fall, and being thus strained, he misses seeing a hole in the pavement and falls headlong. These are actual cases. Yes, the prediction worked. The astrologer has been successful. A surgical operation also may be successful - only the patient died.

What does this all mean? That the *human* element was left out the power of fear. Will the astrologer only crystallize and focalize fear by his forecasts; will he extend the scope of his client's confusion and sense of disorder - or will he be able to give to him who, conciously or subconciously, yearns for guidance into a new realm of order the faith that this new realm exists and can be reached? Will astrology prove an escape into worse confusion, or a technique of integration? It can never be the latter unless the astrologer is fully aware of his personal responsibility *with all necessary means for discharging it.* Which means that the astrologer must be a philosopher and a psychologist - a man of wisdom.

Astrology and Fortune-telling

I wrote that any prediction which does not take *the whole life of a person* as a foundation or frame of reference is incomplete, and often psychologically destructive. The prediction has value only as it contributes to the person's development and essential welfare. Without the recognition of this standard of value the practice of astrology - just as the practice of medicine and psychotherapy - can hardly be justified in a moral or spiritual sense. But in saying this I do not single out the giving of astrological information, freely or with remuneration; for it applies to the imparting of *any* knowledge which refers to the human person.

The matter of "fortune-telling" is only one instance of a much more generalized problem. Fortune-telling is an unorganized attempt at haphazard prediction on the basis of isolated and incomplete data. Its purpose is at best to satisfy the apparent curiosity of the client; at its worst, to pander to his insecurity and his fears for the sake of profit. Even in honest hands and where no monetary transaction is involved, the dangers of fortune-telling are that it is based on the wrong type of psychology, that it singles out for consideration standard matters most likely to impress people's curiosity or vanity, and that it does not seek to contribute to the health or psychological wholeness of the client. Fortune-telling tends to encourage dependence upon external advice and escapism, above all dependence upon external events which are presented as unrelated to the integral life and being of the client. Because the fortune-teller assumes no responsibility for the client's psychological reactions to what is being said - except possibly in the obvious matter of indications of death - he or she also tends to destroy the client's own sense of personal responsibility.

I have said that *events do not happen to us, we happen to them*. An individual person walks - or drifts along collectively determined social paths - toward the future. He meets the vast pageant of universal action and reaction. He meets the world; the world does not bother to go and meet him. If a brick falls upon the man's head as he walks along a street, it is the man's responsibility. *He* walked into the field of the brick's fall. He happened to the brick, because he is a conscious individual and the brick only a piece of universal nature. Man happens to nature. He uses the forces of nature; his, the responsibility for the results. Nature is unconcerned. It merely acts and reacts. It has powers; nay, it *is* power. As one wise man once wrote: "All the powers of nature are there. *Take them*" . . . but if you take them, the results are your responsibility. And if you do not take them, when the time for your own spiritual maturity has come, that also is your responsibility

The astrologer who casts a chart and attempts to solve the problems of his client is using power, power born of the knowledge of the structural pattern of nature as it unfolds through cyclic time. What he does is to relate the client's individual being to his evolving structure of nature - human and universal nature; and relationship always releases power, the power to build or the power to destroy. If the astrologer thinks he merely gives bits of information and then is through with the whole thing, he is greatly mistaken. He has established a relationship. He has placed his client in a new kind of contact or "rapport" with the universe. He has started something vital flowing. To stop there means *unfinished business*. All human tragedies, all apparent accidents, all conflicts are the results of "unfinished business". The astrologer who walks the path of wisdom assesses very highly his responsibility to his ✳ client, and is willing to meet it to the best of his ability and his opportunity. For this reason, he knows how to be silent. Nevertheless, to remain silent when words and knowledge may heal and make whole - that, too, may mean "unfinished business". There is for man no escape from personal responsibility.

THE THIRD STEP

To Establish a Clear Procedure of Work

Having understood the nature and purpose of astrology (first step) and having accepted in advance the responsibility to the client which is inseparable from the wise use of whatever knowledge of the astrological symbols and techniques is to be gained (second step), the would-be astrologer is now ready to take the third step. He (or she) must learn how to establish a clear procedure of work, how to follow a thorough and reliable sequence of operations wich will provide him with the necessary data upon which he can base his psychological interpretations. And first of all, the astrologer must grasp fully the real nature of the tools he is going to use; for every type of activity is always based upon and conditioned by tools, natural or man-made. To act without giving the fullest possible consideration to these tools can only lead to practical inefficiency and mental confusion.

The Astrological Chart as a Symbolical Picture

The first procedure in astrology is always to "erect" or "cast" a chart. An astrological chart can be understood as a kind of chemical formula in which planets and the like represent the simple and basic "elements" which, in their varied combinations, are the subject-matter of the "chemistry" of personality. When thus understood, the chart should make plain to us how every individual, however complex and differentiated in his temperament and behaviour, constitutes actually but a special way of combining factors common to all human beings. The astrological chart is however

28

more than a formula, more than a "map". It is not something merely to be studied with a coldly analytical intellect. It is something to be *felt*.

It should be felt as a living symbol of the whole universe *seen* from a particular place, at a particular time. It is the symbolical representation of one of the most basic human experiences; the experience of the sky, the experience of infinity and order. It is the "Signature" of the Creator, the "musical score" of the universal Harmony which, underneath all storms, all fears and all tumultuous victories, is peace and grandeur. The trained musician looks at the musical score, and he *hears* the tones, with all their moving quality. Likewise, for the trained astrologer, a birthchart should "evoke" the living person; and indeed planets and signs of the zodiac should be seen as actors in a cosmic scene as significant as the religious scenes depicted in countless Crucifixions or Nativities which stir the emotions of the faithful and are symbolical food for the intuition of the wise. The astrological chart is a symbolical picture of a cosmic reality. It should speak to the imagination as much as to the intellect. It should become *alive*.

The Birth-Moment and its Meaning

Every astrological chart is a birth-chart. Astrology has been rightly called "the science of all beginnings" (Marc Jones), because it is based primarily on the study of the *seed-structure of the potentialities of life and of growth made manifest in the first moment of any cycle of organic activity.* The seed is the meeting place of past and future; in it, a cycle comes to its end, and from it, a new cycle emerges. But astrology deals mainly with that aspect of the seed in which the structure of the future organism is revealed as a new and relatively unique set of life-potentialities.

The moment in which the first cry occurs is the significant moment for the erection of a person's chart (horoscope) because it marks the beginning of relatively *independent* existence - and there can be no really new and original set of life-potentialities as long as there is not at least the rudiment of organic independence and expression. The first cry is the first act of integral organic expression, because it is the response of the entire organism to the inrushing air. This inhaled air carries with it the "signature" of the entire past of the universe; but, as the newborn baby releases his first cry, he expresses his original response to the universe. He begins to create his future. This response should normally become increasingly *individual* - a new contribution to life - as the child grows and comes of age; as this occurs, what was at birth only a set of potentialities becomes gradually the concrete actuality of the individual's conscious behaviour and character.

The prenatal stage of organic life is only the summation of the past of the race in anticipation of the time when a present moment, which brings with it the power to begin life (viability), will open the way to the gradual revelation of the future. What we call life is this constant revelation of the future through a series of present situations: a revelation which begins with the first cry.

I should add also that through the first inhalation the rhythm of the blood circulation changes, the blood now passing through and being oxydized within the lungs. Thus it is only then that the heart begins to function in the manner characteristic of a self-sufficient organic whole.

The Birth-Chart and its Elements

While a birth-chart is a two-dimensional graphic representation of the universe as it actually is, this representation is nevertheless a highly selective one. It selects certain factors as "most significant" and leaves out many others - just as a chemical formula stresses a certain type of molecular relationship and ignores many other factors. Astrology selects from all available astronomical data those which fit with certain *"frames of reference"* - and ignores the others.*

* The complete structure of a cycle (for instance, a man's life) from beginning to end is a frame of reference for all moments and all events within the cycle. A house is a frame of reference for estimating the function, meaning, size and value of all the rooms in it. Every factor in human experience can only have meaning if it referred to the larger "structure" of the complete being of the person and of humanity. Thus

The third step

Astrology deals with moving celestial bodies - or more accurately, with the periodic motions of dots and discs of light in the sky. These motions can only be calculated and determined in space and in time when the changing positions of the celestial bodies are measured with reference to either the horizon and the day-period, or the equinoctial positions of the sun within the year cycle, or the relative values of the planets' periods. And these three main frames of reference are known in astrology as the wheel of the Houses, the signs of the zodiac, and the over-all pattern of the solar system (from which the meaning attributed to each planet is derived). Each of these three frames of reference has a very definite character and significance, and in their combination they produce the astrological chart - the one essential tool used in astrology.

The Horizon and the Meridian

The horizon is, generally speaking, the line of the apparent meeting of earth (or sea) and sky. By psychological extension it carries also the meaning of "'the bounds of observation or experience" (Funk and Wagnalls Dictionary). The horizon is the foundation of astrology, because astrology deals with organic wholes, and every organic whole operates within bounds of some sort. Astrology can only deal effectively with specific instances and particular cases. It interprets limitations in terms of their contribution to the wholeness of an organism, or to a well defined situation confronting this organism. Astrology is "the science of all beginnings", because every particular case begins at a particular time, and the nature of the case is seen as symbolically determined or characterized *by the creative potency of life on this globe at this particular time.*

The meridian is the vertical circle which has the polar axis of

what counts most in evaluating or judging the actions of an individual are not the intricate details of the events, but instead the realization of *the way they fit in the framework* of the social, ethical, religious and personal consciousness which is his own and his fellow man's. Even killing may be valued as either an infamous or a glorious action, depending on the occasion, place and time - thus according to the social "frame of reference" used in estimating the meaning and motivation of the act.

the earth as one of its diameters, and on which the Sun is to be found at noon. In this circle is also found the point overhead (the zenith). The line drawn from this point to the center of the earth is the line of gravity, or plumb-line. The horizon and the meridian are always at a 90° angle to each other. As they are prolonged through space they constitute two celestial planes which divide the entire universe into four quarters of equal size. Every celestial object is to be found in one or the other of these quarters.

Projected on paper as two lines, horizontal and vertical, the horizon and meridian form the two main axes of the ordinary astrological chart. These axes constitute the "framework of personality" because all human experiences fall within the basic departments of life they outline. In usual practice each of these four departments of experience is divided into three equal 30° sections *of space* (but not of the zodiac); and thus the twelve houses of the chart are formed.

The Ecliptic

All celestial bodies appear to move in relation to the horizon, and the cyclic period of such a motion is the "sidereal day" of approximately 23 hours and 56 minutes - the period necessary to bring a particular star again over the same meridian. As we study the cyclic motions of celestial bodies with reference to the cross of horizon and meridian,we find however that they come under two basic categories each of which requires a special "frame of reference". The "fixed stars" move through the sidereal day-cycle without changing their mutual relationship in any appreciable manner. But the Sun, the Moon and the planets are in a ceaselessly altered condition of mutual relationship. The patterns they make on the sky change incessantly. It is in order to analyze these changing patterns that the zodiac was devised, as a circle of reference.

The zodiac is the circle described throughout a year by the Sun in its apparent motion in the midst of the "fixed" stars. The Moon and the planets move in various directions and with varying speeds, but they never wander very far on either side of this solar

32

path. It is therefore most convenient to describe their movements in reference to it.

The equator on earth is the greatest circle of terrestrial latitude; but it is considered, besides, as a sort of *global horizon for the human race as a whole.* When indefinitely extended, the plane of the equator crosses the plane formed by the yearly path of the Sun around the sky. The lines formed by their intersection is the *line of equinoxes.* The equinoctial points are the two ends of that line. The point which refers to the positions of the Sun at the beginning of spring in Northern latitudes is taken as the starting point of the circle of longitude - thus as longitude 0°, the "first point of Aries", the conventional beginnig of the zodiac. The circle of longitude is then divided into 360 degrees, and twelve *"signs"* of 30° each: Aries, Taurus, Gemini, Cancer, Virgo, Libra, Scorpio, Sagittarius, Capricorn, Aquarius, Pisces. These signs must not be confused with the constellations of the Greek era which bore, and still bear, the same names. At one time signs and constellations coincided, but now they no longer do, because of a constant drift of the constellations.

The circle of longitude is also called *ecliptic,* because all eclipses occur when the moon is close to it at new moon or full moon. All planetary positions are described in the astrological ephemeris mainly with reference to the ecliptic - in terms of zodiacal longitude and also of celestial latitude (i.e. of their distance north or south from the ecliptic). The relationship between the horizon (at any particular time and place) and the circle of the Sun's yearly journey is also given in terms of the zodiacal longitude of the two ends of the horizon: Ascendant and Descendant. The same is true of the Meridian and of the "cusps" of the twelve houses of the astrological chart.

In some types of astrological computations the positions of celestial bodies are measured with reference to the celestial equator (i.e. instead of the ecliptic), but this is not the most usual method. However "Parallels of declination" are found among the indications listed in most "ephemerides" and astrological magazines.

The Practice of Astrology

The Basic Procedure of Work

The primary data fused by the astrologer are taken from an ephemeris, also from "tables of Houses" calculated by astronomers - they are accurate and scientific facts. They are the raw materials which the astrologer will use in his interpretations. In the astrological technique prevailing today in America these data refer almost entirely to the *longitudes* (or zodiacal positions) of planets and cusps of houses - also of the Moon's nodes; thus to their distance from the equinoxes. The astrology in common use today is an *equinoctial* type of astrology. It is based on the periodical sequence of the seasons - a controlling factor in human life and human culture. What we call the zodiac is actually this cycle of seasons, projected upon the sky.

Many European astrologers, recognizing the dominant meaning of this equinoctial factor, build their astrological charts around it. On the left side of the astrological wheel they place *always* Aries 0°, and every one of the twelve sections correspond to one zodiacal sign. The horizon and meridian at birth are indicated by dotted lines which find their place in these sections according to their longitude. In another type of approach recently popularized - "solar astrology" - the zodiacal degree of the Sun at birth is placed at the left of the wheel, and each section of the wheel contains thirty degrees of the zodiac. Thus, if the natal Sun was located on Cancer 12° the "solar cusps" of this solar birth-chart will be marked with the longitudes Cancer 12°, Leo 12°, Virgo 12°, etc.

These procedures can be justified, yet the charts erected in these ways have the one great fault that they do not map out the universe as it actually appears at the time of birth from the locality of birth. They do not record symbolically *an actual experienceable fact*. The basic fact of birth is that one is born within a particular framework defined by the horizon and meridian. The true "natal horoscope" is a representation of the space around the newborn organism; and the true "natal wheel" is a two-dimensional projection of that space. Its twelve spokes (the cusps of the houses) cut that space at equal angular intervals - but the *zodiacal*

34

> *contents* of these 30° *angles of space* are usually not equal. What
is to be determined first is then how many degrees of the zodiac
are contained in each of these "angles of space" or houses. This is
done by calculating the *sidereal time* of birth and finding out in
the "table of houses" for the geographical latitude of birth the
longitudes of the twelve cusps for that precise time.

I cannot detail here the calculations to be made in order to
determine the positions of the various elements of a birth-chart.
These calculations, and the reasons for them, can be found explained in a great many text-books and manuals for beginners. I shall
merely list the basic operations to be performed, and conclude
with a few general observations the importance of which cannot be
over-estimated.

1. Determine the geographical longitude and latitude of the
birth-place.

2. Determine the "local mean time" of birth. This differs in
most cases from the recorded clock time which is "standard time"
or "Daylight Saving time" - and the difference depends upon the
longitude of birth.

3. Determine the "sidereal time" of birth. This is done by using
as a basis the "sidereal time for Greenwich at noon" recorded for
each day in the ephemeris for the year of birth; then correcting it
according to the exact moment of the "first cry" and the longitude
of birth.

4. Using the "table of houses" for the latitude of birth, find
out the zodiacal positions of the horizon and meridian and of all
twelve house-cusps at the sidereal time of birth - and write these
zodiacal positions exactly where they belong on the birth-chart;
taking care to place accurately the "intercepted signs", if any.

5. Determine the "Greenwich mean time" of birth, noting care-
fully whether the ephemeris used gives the planet's positions for
noon or for midnight.

6. Calculate the zodiacal positions of the Sun, the Moon, the
planets, the Moon Nodes for this Greenwich mean time of birth,

on the basis of the positions recorded in the ephemeris. The use
of logarithms simplifies these calculations if real accuracy is desir-
ed. Special attention should be made to the case of planets having
a retrograde motion.

7. Calculate the position of the "Part of Fortune".

Such are the seven primary steps needed to establish the basic
data which constitute the birth-chart. The following steps deal
with the *organization* of these data in terms of "interpretative
awareness".

A. Outline by appropriate graphic means (for instance with the
use of colored pencils) the pattern of "aspects" made by the planets, and ascertain the basic significance of their over-all configurat-
ion.

B. Determine the "balance in weight" of the planets and their
relative power, individually or in groups, in terms of "dignities"
and house "rulerships". Seek to discover any special type of emphasis, basic pull or center of gravity which could serve as a valid
means to focalize the interpretation and to indicate the main "level" at which the individual naturally functions.

C. Consider one by one the houses of the chart and their planetary and zodiacal contents, relating each to the particular department
of life it symbolizes. Seek to get the "feel" of each planet's activity at the particular place where it is found.

D. Calculate the "progressed positions" of the planets for the
time of the study, and record them on the chart outside of the
natal wheel (with ink or pencil of different color). Calculate the
positions of the planets for the time of the study, and write them
down on the chart, outside of the circle of "progressions" - thus
as "transits". These two types of calculations are valuable even in
the first stage of chart-interpretation for they bring the problem
of interpretation up to an immediate focus of attention. In other
words, the fact that the chart is being studied *at a particular time*
throws light upon the *purpose* of the study - and upon the type

of assistance needed by the client (and it may not be the type he or she "thinks" is needed!)

(E.) With all these data as clearly defined as possible seek to contact in utmost sympathy and understanding the total being of whatever is being represented by the chart - whether it be a living person, or a particular situation. Face the chart as an artist faces a painting, in positive and keenly aware openness to it, with the eager determination to *evoke* the significance of it - and to help the client to reach a fuller state of conscious integration. Face the chart with full acceptation of personal responsibility - and indeed in an attitude of "prayer", asking for inner guidance and the bestowal of wise understanding.

With these five phases of interpretation - to which others should be added as special problems arise and the life of the client has to be studied in detail - we have reached astrological factors which will have to be studied in future chapters. I have listed these phases, nevertheless, in order to establish a preliminary scaffolding (or framework) within which the process of astrological interpretation may operate with a maximum of stability and completeness.

What must be stressed here is the need for clarity and artistry both in actually writing down a chart on paper, and in approaching the problems of interpretation. Every astrologer can devise whatever means seem best to him of making easy the reading of several types of factors in the chart. The symbols, the numbers of degrees, the general disposition of the wheel should be standardized - each astrologer establishing his own standards if necessary. The birth-chart must present itself as a symbol, a living symbol from which the reality of a living person can be evoked. The practice of astrology is an art - and it is also essentially a therapy. Every wise astrologer knows himself to be, whether he likes it or not, an astrotherapist.

THE FOURTH STEP

A Clear Understanding of the Meaning of Zodiacal Signs and Houses

The ordinary astrological text-book makes of the various celestial bodies, whose periodic motions constitute the basic material of astrological interpretation, very definite entities. Indeed we are not so very far in our understanding of the planets from the attitude of ancient astrologers and "star-worshippers". We give masculine or feminine gender to some of these planets. We talk glibly about "my Saturn doing terrible things to me" and the "beautiful Venus". In other words, celestial bodies are understood as yet very nearly as the bodies or "vehicles" of gods whose wills "influence" human affairs - much as the will of a dictator or the religious authority of a pontiff influences the actions of their followers.

Likewise we still consider the zodiacal signs and the houses of the birth-chart as separate entities with absolute prerogatives and set characters, rather than as sections of complete cycles (or circles) having meaning *only as parts of a whole.* This is particularly so with regard to the signs of the zodiac, because the majority of the devotees (and of the critics) of astrology have not yet understood that the signs of the zodiac have nothing to do whatsoever with actual stars and constellations, but are simply twelve phases of the cyclic relationship between the earth and the sun.

However, to be aware of the essential distinction between *constellations* which are groups of actual stars, and *signs of the zodiac* which are twelve divisions of the ecliptic (apparent path of the sun, or circle of longitude) is not enough. The type of understanding and "astrological wisdom" which I am presenting requires that we realize clearly a more basic principle: the principle of the *priority of the whole over the parts of this whole.*

What this practically means is that the yearly path of the sun comes first, the twelve signs of the zodiac afterwards; that these signs have meaning only in terms of their place within the ecliptic as a whole. It means that each house of the chart is significant because it is a particular expression of the total space surrounding a man living on the surface of our globe - a space inevitably divided into two halves (soil and sky) by the horizon. A house is a section of either the soil-space or the sky-space, and its significance can be determined by the fact that it precedes and follows other houses; that is to say, it has significance as one factor in a cyclic series of factors.

The meaning of the planets has, according to my astrological outlook, no different foundation. Each planet acquires its meaning because of the fact that it occupies a particular place in the sequence of planets which develops on either side of the earth's orbit. Mars represents what it does in astrology because it is the planet next to the earth *outside* of our orbit; Venus because it is the planet next to the earth *inside* our orbit. This is the one fundamental meaning of Mars and Venus - and similarly of any other planet. What is *first* is the solar system as a whole. This whole has a typical structure defined by the relation of its parts to the whole, and of each part to every other part. And as we, earth-beings, are the ones who are studying and giving meaning to this solar-system-whole, we have obviously to refer whatever meaning we attribute to any part of the whole *to ourselves.** We therefore give meaning to the planets-series with reference to the earth as a point of de-

---

* Even in so-called "heliocentric astrology" one is still referring the positions of the planets and of everything else to ourselves, earth-beings; but instead of dealing with the earth as a solid object, or with one's position on the earth, one deals (as I have explained elsewhere) with the *orbit of the earth as a whole.* The Sun is taken as the "center" of that orbit and thus serves as a projected center of measurement, but the real frame of reference is the orbit as a whole.

parture - just as we say that Aries has a particular character in the cyclic zodiacal series because it is the first sign after the vernal equinox; Taurus, because it is the second sign, etc.

But the qualifications "first", "second", "third", etc. are purely abstract; and we would present astrology, as a "technique of human understanding", in a wrong light if we were to think of it *merely* as a kind of numerology. Astrology, I repeat, is based upon the common experience of human beings and upon the most basic response of man to the one fundamental fact of human existence: the contrast between earth and sky - between the chaos of earth-experiences and the majestic order of the realm of moving celestial lights.

Primitive astrology stressed this basic response and built upon it in the only way possible to primitive mentality; that is, by making of everything celestial an entity - a god, a place, a "house", a solid and personal thing. But with the advent of a new era of mental development in, or before, the sixth century B.C. (the time of Pythagoras) men began - oh! very hesitantly - to think in terms of series and cycles instead of "gods" and Powers; and a new astrology was born, but never grown to maturity.

It is this "new" astrology to which we should now at last give fuller mature expression, free from the old Ptolemaic compromises with archaic tradition. And the only way I know to establish this fully mature approach to astrology is to start from the realization that the *whole is prior to the parts, in potentiality and in meaning.* The tree and all its parts originate in the seed; all the wonderfully complex organs of the human body are *specialized divisions* of a primordial fecundated ovum. Likewise the signs of the zodiac are "specialized divisions" of the space surrounding any man on earth; and the planets are specialized "organs" of the solar-system-whole. We are not adding up liver, stomach, heart, brain to make man. We likewise should not add up separate planetary entities to make up the solar system - or the various factors found in a birth-chart in order to build up a composite judgment. We should seek to understand the whole on its plane of operative wholeness, and the parts will reveal their functional meaning to our mind through a natural process of progressive unfoldment and rhythmic accentuation. The knowledge thus gained will be *functional* knowledge, not abstractly intellectual - and wisdom is to functional knowledge what flowers are to leaves. Within the flower the new seed comes to birth; likewise, out of wisdom meaning arises. And meaning, once formulated, becomes the creative power, the Word or *Logos*. The true astrologer is he who can "evoke" in his mind the meaning of a chart; and as he formulates this meaning through adequate words he releases creative power, the power to bring to his client a greater sense of life, personality, integration and happiness. A rarely reached goal, indeed - yet the ultimate goal of all truly valid astrological interpretation.

The Zodiac and the Circle of Houses

The zodiac and the circle of the twelve houses are two basic frames of reference which have many things in common; nevertheless, they must be clearly differentiated in the mind of the student of astrology if his or her interpretation is not to lack sharpness and real validity. Zodiacal signs and houses have in common the fact that they are considered usually as spatial factors; that is, they are said to constitute compartments inside of which celestial bodies are located - these bodies acquiring thereby special colorations or characteristic traits, and being strengthened or weakened in their action. There are moreover twelve signs and twelve houses, and the two series give rise to similar sequences of features and meanings. Thus Aries, being the first sign, has characteristics which parallel those of the first house of an astrological chart; Cancer, being the fourth sign parallels in meaning the fourth house, etc.

This is so evident in the usual astrological teaching that the signs of the zodiac have been called at times the "houses of the Sun", and also they are considered as the day or night "mansions" of the planets. Religiously minded astrologers, indeed, refer to the zodiacal signs as the "many mansions" in the Father's house, of which Jesus speaks in the Gospels. The zodiac as a whole has been

41

interpreted as a kind of "aura", or electro-magnetic spheroid, surrounding the earth, each sign representing a section of this aura. Also correspondences have been established traditionally between each sign and a part of the human body - the whole zodiac being said to represent the body of the macrocosmos, or Heavenly Man.

This spatial interpretation of the zodiac is entirely justifiable, and I have developed some of its features in my book "The Pulse of Life". But if this point of view is taken, it must be made clear that space, in relation to the zodiac, is of an entirely different order from the space with which the houses deal. The zodiac is a "universal matrix" - thus a *place;* yet a matrix is not an ordinary kind of space. It is an electro-magnetic "field" upon which formative Powers are focused. It is living substance in the process of being built into an organism. It is not a "house" or a collection of neatly defined spaces, but the *crucible of life.*

The zodiac is the formative realm of life in which the astrological Sun operates as the fountain-head of all life-processes. It is the realm of birthing, growing, maturing, decaying and dying; where substance is made and unmade; where anabolic and catabolic forces (light and shadow, integration and disintegration) operate in intense, unceasing, dynamic being. We can think of a sign of the zodiac as a region in which one aspect of the solar force is concentrated in work; but if we picture this place in static terms we are greatly mistaken. The essence of the zodiac is dynamic activity at the level of the formation of substance, of polar electro-magnetic energies, of life-processes. The Sun is the inexhaustible power which makes that activity possible; the planets differentiate it along functional lines in obedience to definite structural patterns. And the zodiac is the field in and through which all this activity operates as energy-substance. It is the "astral world" of the earlier Theosophical books (for instance, of "Light on the Path") - the world of forces, the active-generative aspect of Nature. And the ancients correlated each sign of the zodiac with a Celestial Hierarchy, a Host of cosmic Builders.

Thus to say that the sign Taurus corresponds to the neck in the human body is misleading. The sign "rules" the vital functions, the field of operation of which is the neck. Taurus energizes, solarizes, ensouls even, the neck and its organs (for instance the thyroid gland and the vocal cords). But Taurus *is not* the neck. Taurus represents a phase of solar activity. It is a form of power, an aspect of life. The activity or release of formative energy is the essential factor; the place at which this release of energy is focalized is of secondary importance.

This explains why a sign of the zodiac cannot be permanently associated with a group of stars (constellation); and it indicates the way in which the precession of the equinoxes and the series of the twelve great Ages (Arian, Piscean, Aquarian, etc.) operate. Everything in the universe acts under the principle of "permutation of functions". Every place can and must, in due time, become the focal fields for the operation of *all* conceivable life-functions or cosmic activities. The Aries function at one time is focused (symbolically or cosmically) upon the group of stars named the Ram, at another time upon the constellation of the Fishes, later on that of the Water-Bearer. The *function* - the zodiacal sign - is the basic thing; the *purpose* and the *agencies* through which it works are, in a sense, secondary - they are symbolized by the actual star-groups or constellations.

To use another example: John F. Kennedy dies, Lyndon B. Johnson comes to the White House - but the Executive function of the Presidency is the basic factor. This function, at one time, could best be worked out through a man of Kennedy's type (a particular star-group), at another through a man of Johnson's type (another star-group). And, as a result, we have a succession of precessional Ages, each lasting some 2100 years. The signs of the zodiac are "offices" of the government; the governing power is the Sun. The Presidency is an "office" - but it should not be identified too closely with a structure or place, the White House. It is a function, not a place in space.

On the other hand when we come to the houses of the astrological chart we are dealing actually with sections of a most concrete types of space. The horizon circle (which becomes the lines linking the Ascendant and the Descendant in the two-dimensional astrological chart) divides the space surrounding the native (the person whose chart is being studied) into two halves or hemispheres. One half is sky; the other, solid earth. The division is factual, concrete, inescapable - as the distinction between day and night. The difference between signs of the zodiac is a matter of *plus* and *minus*, of relative preponderance between two polar energies both of which are always present everywhere, at any time. But sky and earth are complete opposites; they are different places, which can merge only within a very narrow fringe - this fringe being the surface of the earth, the birth-place of consciousness; and thus the line of Ascendant-Descendant represents consciousness, with its subjective and objective poles.

It is indeed essential to grasp the meaning of the difference between these two wholes, the zodiac and the circle of houses, for both are often quite misunderstood. I have discussed the meaning of houses in many magazine articles, and all that I shall say here is that the houses represent the twelve kinds of experiences which a particular human being meets *as he moves about in space,* and meeting which he becomes in fact an "individual".

Man moves about in space: this is his basic prerogative. The ability to displace oneself does not exist in the vegetable kingdom. It develops through the animal kingdom. It is perfected in the human kingdom; first, through muscles, then through machines, finally through the development of more specialized mental-spiritual powers. It is by displacing himself that man becomes truly individualized. He leaves his ancestral home, his birth-place, his country - and at every step he becomes more of an "individual self". Self-development is based on the power constantly to reorient oneself in space - literally, to find "a new orient". Reorientation, in this deeper sense, means to see the self (the Ascendant, or Eastern horizon) from a new point of view in space. Man moves thus from house to house, and as he does so he sees himself - and the outher world (Descendant) - differently.

How does one move from house to house? Simply by shifting the main focus of one's attention from one department of human experience to another. Each house represents a basic department of experience, and thus the *potentiality* of a different type of consciousness. Indead the circle of houses refers primarily to consciousness, and basic changes in consciousness; and it is essentially an expression of a *changing horizon*. The horizon travels around the heavens once every day. Likewise an individual can only find himself in the fullness of his power and humanity if he travels around himself and around his world. And *potentially* every single 24-hour period gives a man a chance to perform such a global journey. The alternation of day and night, and the regular series of daily activities, normally compel the fully alive individual, to come in touch with all the basic facets of his being and to operate on all the levels of consciousness, from deepest sleep to most active wakefulness.

Every day the Sun moves through all twelve houses, giving to man the power to function through each and all. The astrologer marks on the cusps of the twelve houses of his chart a particular sign and degree of the zodiac. But what these zodiacal indications refer to, essentially, is the position of the Sun above or below the horizon. The sign and degree of the zodiac simply add more detail to this basic indication - and it also reveals the particular latitude at which the person operates, which again affects his ability to receive the Sun's energy.

The zodiac is nothing but a multiple expression of solar activity - a way of measuring the character of this activity at any time. But the position of the Sun in a house indicates the *place* upon which this solar power is focused - and the position of the planets in the house enables us also to locate the main foci of planetary operations (which *differentiate* solar activity for the sake of more intricate and subtle functioning).

If this fundamental distinction between zodiac and circle of houses is well understood, there can be no difficulty in grasping the detailed meaning of each sign and each house. The parts display the essential characteristics of the whole; but no one can truly realize the significance of any part without being imbued with the meaning of the whole. Every house of a chart refers to a type of *consciousness* to be gained by orienting oneself through space while performing the everyday activities of personal and social living. And every zodiacal sign is an expression of the *power* to live and to experience, which has its source in the Sun.

The Sun's energy (light) reflects and deflects off the other planets creating a living matrix, as in a gene, indicative of the Native's life or modus operendi.

THE FIFTH STEP

The Use of the "Lights"

To speak of the zodiac as "the formative realm of life in which the Sun operates as the fountainhead of all life-processes" does not sufficiently reveal the essential character of solar activity. What the Sun releases is not "life", but "light" - better still, it is the capacity to produce definite effects in whatever substance is touched by the sun-rays. These effects can be classified into various categories. As we experience them on the surface of the earth they are of three fundamental types.

First, we can speak of *sunlight* and of its power to illumine us and to reveal the presence, shape and color of physical substances, bodies and objects. This is the most direct (or directly apprehended) effect of solar activity upon human beings - and as well upon other organisms. Then, there is *solar heat* which, as it warms all living creatures, makes their existence possible. Heat, however, is not a direct product of solar activity. There is practically no heat in inter-stellar space, and the generation of heat depends greatly upon the condition of the tenuous substances which surround the earth-surface.

The surrounding regions of our solid globe - the realm of air, of clouds and of ionized layers above the stratosphere - were named by the ancient astrologers-astronomers - the "sublunar realm". In that realm the Moon ruled supreme and, by the control of heat (and even of the intensity of light) through moisture and clouds, the Moon was understood to exercise dominion over the generation and the tidal flow of *life*. This dominion was particularly ef-

47

fective at the dawn of life on the earth, when the earth's surface was wrapped in a thick, unbroken envelope of fog and clouds. Light, then, had to seep through this lunar envelope and, thus, could be experienced only in an indirect manner, through the intermediary of the lunar realm and its forces.

When at long last - early during the fabled "Atlantean" period - the fog-envelope broke and the sun-disc could be seen directly as a well-defined fountainhead of light, and the Moon also appeared in the clear night-sky, presenting the puzzling spectacle of her periodical phases to primitive man, then, the dualism of the solar and the lunar "Lights" became the very foundation of nascent astrology, and as well of all mythologies and cosmologies. Two basic types of cosmic activities came to be recognized: solar activity became the mark of creative "spirit", while lunar activity became linked with the generation and dissolution of "life" in earthly bodies.

Solar spirit is the polar opposite of substance-energy, and the signs of the zodiac refer to the twelve basic types into which this universal and protean energy-substance is polarized by solar activity. The Moon in astrology does not deal directly with substance itself - with electrons, atoms and molecules - but instead with the generation of living organisms, of species, *genera* and races. "Life" is the power which forms characteristic organic structures giving them the ability to adapt themselves to their respective environments. Some philosophers today call this power "creative evolution". Men of old thought of it as the great lunar god, *the Demiurge* (Jehovah among the Gnostics), the builder of the material universe of living bodies.

A clear understanding of the fundamental values demonstrated by these two orders of activity, solar and lunar, is essential to the astrologer. This understanding should include a thorough grasp of the historical process which led humanity to establish, as a result of its collective experience, the basis for this celestial symbolism. It should include also a psychological study of the power wielded by these two great "primordial Images" - the Sun and Moon as

48

sources of "light" and "life" - within the collective Unconcious of all men. Only on such a basis can astrology perform its work of personal integration, by enabling the mature individual to assimilate and make his own the truly cosmic energies latent in man's common humanity - in *human* nature.

The Sun as "Potential" of Life and Selfhood

The rays of the Sun can be as much a cause of death as of life. They constitute a possibility of life; but, unless they are intimately associated with some other factors, life cannot manifest. Sunlight likewise is a potentiality of vision and consciousness; but, unless special organic structures are built to receive the light-rays, there can be no seeing. Solar activity spreads out in space, indifferently and universally. It stirs everything it touches - provided there is some agency able to absorb, assimilate and differentiate it for use. One can thus compare the Sun to the fuel on which an engine runs; if a person is born with the Sun in Taurus, it means that the "engine" of this man's body and psyche (his total personality) operates essentially by consuming a Taurus type of bio-psychological energy (or "fuel").

The best kind of fuel will often not improve the performance of a poorly built, defective or worn out engine; in fact it usually will tend to accelerate the break-down process, or cause the engine to explode. Hundred per cent octane gas is only a potentiality of speed. It becomes the source of actual speed only if a resistant motor with a high capacity for releasing power is built.

Likewise the place of the Sun in an astrological chart is no guarantee of actual life; it defines merely a certain type of potentiality of life-characteristics. And at the psychological-mental, or "spiritual" level, the Sun refers also merely to the capacity of developing a particular type of selfhood in reference to a particular kind of purpose. The potency of that purpose, as it pulls the personality towards its realization, is what we call "will". The Sun represents the self, the purpose and the will of a person - but only in their latent or undifferentiated state, as spiritual "potential" and virgin

49

substance-energy. Actual performance will come as this substance-energy is captured and transformed into a simple oscillatory activity with waxing and waning phases, or into some still more complex type of group-operation. The first alternative refers to the Moon; the second, to the combined cycles of all planets of the solar system.

The Moon as "Builder" of the Structures of Life and Consciousness

What we usually call life is the capacity in an organism to maintain and reproduce its structural characteristics and its functional rhythms. This capacity operates generically, rather than individually, and mainly as an unconscious factor. It operates, in all advanced stages of evolution, through the kind of polar dualism which can be called "sex", using the term in its broadest sense. This polar dualism is expressed very significantly in astrology by the symbolism of the two Lights - the Sun and the Moon. The former is the animating, fecundating principle; the latter represents the receptive and generative pole, which is characterized by its changeable, oscillating character.

The main function of the Moon is to deal with the element of solar *heat* and to use it in conjunction with the element of *moisture*. Organic life depends upon the polar interplay of these two elements. The "moisture" of the so-called "sub-lunar regions" around the solid globe of the earth captures the solar power as heat, and, as the tidal rhythm of the Moon operates, this solar power is distributed through the ready substance of the earth; and the need of the earth for like-kingdoms is fulfilled in the generation of cells and bodies.

This may seem a very un-scientific way of dealing with the subject of life on the earth, but it is the traditional way of astrological symbolism, and a very significant one. It applies to the psychological-mental level in man as well as to the purely biological-physical realm. The Moon, at the psychological-mental level, represents the "moisture" in man's inner nature; that is, the generative factor of

50

feeling. And it is out of the structures built by the feelings that the consciousness of individual selfhood emerge ... for better or for worse!

This last statement may seem puzzling to people who have been trained in the belief that consciousness and selfhood were of a mental nature. Such a belief, however, has no foundation in the realm of duality which is, strictly speaking, the realm of life. In that realm everything depends upon the polar dualism of solar and lunar activity. In it, "mind" operates as the power of adaptation to experience; and it is actually an extension and abstract development of the capacity for feeling - *which is the capacity to generate structures of consciousness.* The ego is the most basic of these structures - thus, the astrological connection between the Moon and the ego, between the "lunar" nature and man's "personal" behavior. Psychological complexes, seen from this point of view, are likewise lunar structures of consciousness; they are closely related to frustrations and repressions in the flow of the organic rhythm of the instincts, and particularly of those related directly or indirectly to the sexual functions.

The feelings are psychological expressions of biological instincts, which in truth are waves and eddies in the tidal flow of the lunar forces acting upon the "moisture" in man's body and psyche. This tidal flow is represented in astrology by the lunation cycle and the phases of the Moon. These phases are not to be understood as changes in the Moon herself as a celestial globe, but as *changes in the relationship of the Moon to the Sun.*

What the lunation cycle measures are the polar ebbs and flows of solar heat within the lunar "moisture", the expansion and contraction of the generative forces. And these forces generate (or build) psychological structures as well as biological ones. They give birth to the personal ego (a structure of consiousness born of individualized feelings) as well as to the delicate balance of the endocrine glands in the body - a balance which is based on definite (though changing) patterns in the "lunar body" of the individual (the astral body mentioned in modern occultism).

The feelings are the reactions of the organism-as-a-whole to human experience - inner as well as outer experience. And this organism-as-a-whole functions at first, and basically, through all the *fluids* of the body - blood and lymph, and all the secretions of the glands. It has been said that man's body is for the most part sea water. All living creatures were born of the sea; and the sea is the vast reservoir of primordial, undifferentiated substances from which all relatively separate organisms and organic structures have emerged. It is thus the symbol of the collective Unconscious, the reservoir in which all common factors and common reactions of men have their origin, and also to which they return as sub-merged memories and instinct-patterns. Likewise man's inner nature is for the most part feelings; and these feelings constitute the "liquid" element (moisture or water) which is sea, lake, river, well, to the individual consciousness and the ego. The rise of cultures and civilizations and all primary modes of human exchange, commerce and travel, are dependent upon the presence and utilization of water by mankind; and similarly an individual's psychological reactions, mental images and thought structures are born out of feelings. They are transmitted in their *vital* state through *consciously formulated feelings* (symbols and words able to arouse other men's organic responses and emotions).

The Sun provides the original vibratory impulse, the fecundating rhythm or "tone". The solar power goes forth in answer to the *need* of the earth and all material substances which, as disintegrated remains of the past, yearn to be able once more to experience organic wholeness and spirit. But these inchoate materials are not able to receive *directly* the power of the Sun, or the vision and the creative idea that emanate from the spiritual source. It is thus the Moon's task to receive this fecundant power from the Sun at the new moon, and, through the waxing period of the lunation, to build instrumentalities and organs which will be able to receive and to retain the solar impulse, idea or purpose. This reception occurs, symbolically, at the full moon, when the disc of the Moon reflects in full the disc of the Sun. Thereafter, as the light of the Moon wanes, this light is symbolically absorbed by the earth-creatures; the realization of the solar idea and purpose becomes part and parcel of the men and minds who receive it at the full moon. They assimilate it as concepts and thoughts; they extract from it meaning; and this meaning becomes formulated through words and symbols, which serve to build the conscious fabric of human civilization - or, in the life of the mature and spiritually evolved individual, the warp and woof of his immortal "spiritual body" victorious over physical disintegration and death.

The Horizon and the "Lights"

The need of the earth and of all its inhabitants is the fundamental factor which brings sense and purposefulness to the cyclic interplay of the solar and lunar forces. The Moon is the servant of the earth in that she provides earth creatures with the organic structures (biological and psychological) which they need in order to assimilate the light of the Sun. And the Sun himself, as seen in relation to the zodiac (that is, to the orbital revolutions of the earth) has meaning in terms of the power he releases for the sake of the earth.

The earth is thus the basis for the soli-lunar activity; and in the birth-charts of individuals, this basis appears as the horizon-line, linking the Ascendant (East) and the Descendant (West). The positions of the Sun and the Moon in relation to the horizon are thus of primary importance, especially in all matters which deal with life and with man's fundamental capacity to experience and to feel as an organic entity. This capacity in turn manifests as the ability shown by an individual human being to radiate what is called today "personality" and to enjoy happiness.

Four essential combinations of horizon, Sun and Moon are possible.

1. *Sun above and Moon below the horizon:* The horizon is the "axis of consciousness" which separates the subjective realm of individual being (the solid earth) from the objective world of social

and collective existence (the sky above). Therefore in this first soli-lunar combination the life of the human being is lived *primarily* through inner and individualized structures (the Moon) which reveal a collective, racial or social purpose (the Sun). Throughout his life and especially in time of crisis the person tends to give an individual form to a racial-social purpose or a collective ideal. Examples: Napoleon I, Nietzsche, Walt Whitman, Einstein, Henry Ford.

2. *Sun below and Moon above the horizon:* Life, in this instance is lived primarily in order to give a collective, social expression to an individualistic purpose or will. In this as in the first case, a definite dualism of consciousness is shown. It may make for a balanced life in which the inner and the outer realms of being cooperate rhythmically; but it may also indicate a basic psychological conflict between "solar" and "lunar" forces, between spiritual purpose and personal desire. Examples: F. D. Roosevelt, Count Hermann Keyserling, Wendell Wilkie, George Bernard Shaw, Luther Burbank.

3. *Sun and Moon above the horizon:* The main focus of the life is in the outer world. Both the essential purpose and the characteristic bio-psychological traits of the individual are polarized by racial, cultural, social ideals or collectively spiritual values. Examples: Washington, Gandhi, Mussolini, Karl Marx, Czar Nicholas II, Richard Wagner.

4. *Sun and Moon below the horizon:* Life is lived, in this case, from the inner, subjective center in order primarily to fulfill the will and purpose of the self, and by means of predominantly individualistic structures of behavior, thought and feelings. This may lead to introversion and self-centeredness, or creative originality. Examples: Cromwell, Robespierre, Chopin, Liszt, Pope Pius XII, Lenin, Stalin.

Another way of reaching an interpretation of the positions of the Sun and the Moon with reference to the horizon is the study of the "Part of Fortune" as an index to the individual's capacity for happiness and ease in relationship, and as a result, for social success. The Part of Fortune's position in the houses of the chart depends upon the phase of the Moon, thus, upon the angular relationship between the Sun and the Moon. It is below the horizon during the waxing period of the lunation; and above the horizon as the moon decreases in light.*

* For a detailed study of the cyclic relationship of the Moon to the Sun, and of the Part of Fortune, read my book, "The Lunation Cycle".

THE SIXTH STEP

The Study of the Planetary System as a Whole

The Planets and the Sun

I t has become the custom in modern astrology to link together under the name of "planets" every moving celestial body belong-
ing to our solar system, including the Sun and the Moon. This
practice derives largely from the use of the ephemeris in which the
positions of the Sun, the Moon and the planets are listed side by
side, and it has obviously some degree of justification. Yet the
ancient astrologers were wise indeed in establishing a very clear
distinction between the two Lights (Sun and Moon) and the planets themselves. I repeat that the Lights refer to the realm of life
proper - a realm of duality and of polar interplay between two
basic types of forces or factors (solar and lunar); a realm which
reveals the foundations of the very process of living, and the meaning or purpose of this universal process. The Sun represents the
spiritual purpose which calls every living organism into being, and
the orginal impulse (or release of life-*potential*) which is the
fountain-head of all the energies which will animate this organism;
while the Moon symbolizes those evolutionary forces which successively generate, illumine and disintegrate the generic and racial form of the organism, building and destroying cells and organs
through which the solar potential can become actualized as biol-
ogical-psychological activity. These solar and lunar factors are directed toward the fulfillment of the *need* of earth-substance which,
through their activity, is once more enabled to experience life and

the state of organic wholeness or spiritual integration.

We are thus primarily dealing with three inseparable factors: - Sun, Moon and earth (the latter becoming the horizon-line in individual birth-charts). They constitute "reality" - the whole of it - at the level of life pure and simple. Nothing needs fundamentally to be added to them. The Sun is "purpose"; the Moon is "life". The periodical relationship of the Moon and the Sun (the lunation cycle) reveals the "purpose of living" (the solar value of the Moon's activity) and as well the special or individual character of the will to live (the lunar expression of the solar purpose). This will to live (the essence of all bio-psychological activity) is, on the one hand, the *potency of purpose,* and on the other, the *feeling-reactions* to the life-forces out of which consciousness and selfhood emerge. Indeed, this realm of life *per se* is, in every one of its aspects, the realm of duality. It is the world of polarity, of sex, of "personality" (the radiance, or heaviness, of bio-psychological living), of happiness - and of drama born of conflicts.

There is, however, another realm of human development; one which is governed no longer by duality, but instead by the principle of *multiple functional integration.* It is the realm in which the solar system as a whole operates, conditioning at every moment - through its interplanetary structure - the *tone-quality* of the solar releases of life-potential and purpose. These solar releases fecundate the lunar sphere and arouse in it the evolutionary energies which actually construct the body (and later the psychological structures) of the human individual. However, as these lunar builders evolve the cells and organs of the man-to-be, they follow *unconsciously* the pattern latent in the solar release, or "tone". They do so in the manner (as yet most mysterious to us) in which the acorn grows into the oak tree, bringing out into manifestation as roots, trunk, leaves, flowers the structures which the seed somehow contained as *life-potential.*

This life-potential - this seed-pattern - is projected or emanated, by the creative spirit (the Sun, in astrology); *but it is determined or conditioned* by the state of the solar system as a whole - thus, by the complex relationships of the planets to the Sun and to each other. To think that a planet, individually and separately, influences an organism on the earth-surface by sending some mysterious kind of "ray" ... is probably naive. What "influences" the formation, generation and development of earth-creatures is the *total state of the solar system* during every phase of the life-process - and especially as the human being reaches, with the first breath, the condition of independent existence. This "total state of the solar system" acts in a direct way *only through the Sun,* source of all life-processes. But what is released by the Sun is given archetypal form or "tone-quality" by the solar system as a whole - thus, by the assembly of the planets. We might say that the planets constitute (approximately) the Legislature while the Sun is the Executive; in which case we would have to think of the Moon as the many governmental agencies and managerial bureaux bringing laws and executive decisions down to the level of actual practical application and concrete management.

Solar releases can be likened to instrumental tones, each of which represents a complex grouping of secondary vibrations or "overtones". The *inner structure* of these tones (which gives them their individual character, rhythm and quality) is symbolized in astrology by the planetary structure of the birth-chart. The Sun represents the purpose of a life; but every effective purpose is conditioned by a plan of operation. The purpose determines the plan; yet the purpose is also conditioned by the actual possibility there is of making a workable plan to realize this purpose - much as musical tones are conditioned by the limitations of the instruments. The planets, considered as a group, constitute the workable plan, and as well those agencies which oversee its workings.

How to Determine the Meaning of the Planets

When asked how the various planets came to receive the meaning and characteristics attributed to them in astrology, most astrologers are likely to say that these planetary characteristics are the results of centuries and millennia of observations in which connections between planetary positions, events and personal characteristics were tested out and established by repeated evidence. Astrology, however, can present only very uncertain claims - historically as well as philosophically - to the status of a "science" as this term is understood today. It has, in fact, a much more significant position within the vast field of human knowledge and wisdom than that of an immature and far from exact emperical science. I defined astrology as a technique in human understanding and said that its essential method is to go from *the whole to the parts;* thus, for instance, from the entire yearly path of the Sun to the twelve component zodiacal signs, from the space surrounding the newborn to the twelve houses which are specialized divisions of this space. Likewise as we come to analyze the individual significance of the planets in astrology we should follow the same method and consider first of all the solar system as a whole, as a cosmic organism in which every planet (and planetoid, if need be) occupies a particular place and fulfills a particular function.

As the zodiacal signs Aries and Gemini possess certain essential characteristics because of being respectively the first and third signs which follow the spring equinox (the beginning of the "natural zodiac"), likewise, the basic meaning of every planet - *for us human beings* - is derived from the planet's place within the total structure of the solar system *as seen and understood by men.* This meaning is determined by the order of the planets in the two planetary series extending from the earth to the Sun, and from the earth to the outer spaces of the galaxy. Thus the astrological significance of Venus is a consequence of the fact that Venus is the first planet in the series which reaches Sun-ward; while Mars, being the first planet in the planetary sequence in the direction of galactic spaces, is thereby endowed with an opposite and complementary attribute. After Venus, in the direction of the Sun, comes Mercury. This fact serves to establish Mercury's fundamental characteristics; while the belt of asteroids separating Mars from Jupiter and Saturn establishes a basic distinction between the former and the two giants of the solar system.

The size of the planet, the peculiarities of its motions, the number of its satellites and their peculiarities of motion, add also a great deal to our understanding of the planet's "function" within the solar system - as *we* experience it. From all these data the essential significance and the characteristic attributes of every planet (even of those very recently discovered) are derived by a deductive process which is an expression of this capacity for "functional knowledge" which I already mentioned as the outstanding manifestation of astrological wisdom.

The planets can be likened to pattern-making agencies impressing their group-decisions upon the basic types of energies which flow constantly from the Sun. Let me repeat that the planets do not themselves release energy; but they act, in astrological symbolism, as if they activated, accentuated or attenuated, those life-forces with they have an "affinity". Mars, for instance, does not "generate" what human beings experience as desire, or initiative, or aggressiveness. This type of power streams from the Sun, together with other kinds of power; but because Mars is the planet next to, and outside of, the earth's orbit, Mars becomes invested with the characteristics of out-going initiative and impulsive desire *in so far as earth creatures are concerned*.

Saturn is likewise, to all organisms on the earth, the symbolic expression of the power of contraction and limitation, because it succeeds the expansive Jupiter in the planetary series - Jupiter, which takes the raw Martian impulsiveness and matures it within the matrix of social relationship and group-responsibility. But Mars, Jupiter, Saturn, or any other planet, do not generate life-power. They simply act as "transformers" of the complex solar energy; separating, as it were, the several basic energy-threads and giving to each the special intensity and character which belongs to it according to an overall pattern or plan - indeed, the very pattern revealed by the grouping of the planets themselves in the sky at the moment of birth.

The action of the planets could perhaps best be illustrated symbolically by that of a prism which separates the different colors contained in the solar light, and spreads them in space according to a definite pattern (the spectrum of sunlight). The nearly concentric orbits of the planets would act as a diffraction grating (an instrument which can take the place of a prism in physics) dispersing or differentiating sunlight, resolving it into component energies. Each planet would thus correspond to a certain color of the spectrum, according to its place in the "grating" of the solar system. But one apparently should not use this analogy in order to connect every planet with a particular color as the planetary sequence does not follow the color scale.

Because such an interpretation of the function of the planets in astrology is rather abstract, the astrologer has been more or less compelled to speak in semi-mythological terms, and to make of every planet an entity with the power to "influence" earthly organisms and human minds - indeed, a sort of god. Yet it is time for all thinking persons interested in astrology to ask for an interpretation which considers the planets not as separate Powers, decreeing good fortune or tragedy for men, but as a group of factors - a collective instrumentality - which takes the complex, but latent, power of the Sun's light, differentiates and spreads it out into colored rays, each of which performs a particular function in the body and psyche of human beings. The planets are not the "rays", but the *indicators of the process* which differentiates solar light into "rays" or modes of organic power at work.

Planetary Classifications

This process of differentiation, then of focalization upon the various parts of the living organism (produced by the generative power of the Moon) can be divided into several phases. The character of these phases is revealed symbolically through the different ways in which planets can be paired, or linked in groups. And it is only as one fully understands these various types of inter-planetary relationships that the astrological meaning of each and all planets becomes a *living reality* in the consciousness of the astrologer.

In one of these types of inter-planetary relationships the planets are paired by their rank in the two series which lead in opposite directions away from the earth: thus Mars and Venus, Jupiter and Mercury and the outer Sun (which may stand, in this case, for an intra-Mercurial planet, Vulcan). This pairing is very significant - but less in the popular way in which Mars represents the masculine and Venus the feminine poles of sexuality, than in the deeper sense of the universal balance between *centrifugal* (Mars, as head of the outer series of planets) and *centripetal* forces (Venus as head of the inner, Sun-ward series). Indeed, the meaning of his Mars-Venus polarization is the meaning of "outward"; and "inward"; and these two directions of growth or unfoldment are found wherever there is life and consciousness.

That there is such a two-fold polarization of the basic solar potential is the first fact to consider in the study of the planets; Mars and Venus are the primary and most personal expressions of that fact. They represent the most intimate realization of duality known to a human being. Such a realization, however, does not come to a human being as a result of successive changes from one polarity to another. It is not the realization of this, then that; but of this *and* that - both at the same time. In the realm of lunar generation there is an alternation of polarities: one type of activity follows another periodically. But when we deal with the realm of planets we deal with *simultaneous* modes of activities. The lunar world is the world of duration, of duality experienced in successive phases. The planetary world is the realm of "multiple functional integration"; planets operate all the time, even though the *relative intensity* of the planets' activities is constantly modified (this being shown in astrology by their "dignities", that is, their positions in zodiacal signs and houses).

This difference between the lunar and the planetary realms is of capital importance. Where *succession of changes* in the process of life is the basic fact, consciousness is in bondage to time. But where *simultaneity of expression* exists - where one factor wanes while another waxes, and all factors balance and interpenetrate each other in a multitude of ways - there, consciousness is able to perpetuate itself and to establish its own stable vehicle of expression. In such a vehicle, the individual selfhood of a man or of a group of men is retained, sustained and reproduced.

Where a group of men is concerned, such a vehicle of expression is a "culture" and the sum-total of the creations inspired by the group's typical response to life experiences. In the case of an individual person, the selfhood of that person can become immortalized within the "spiritual body", of which mystics and occultists speak, and which can be considered as a planetary web of solar energies established at the level of the creative-dynamic mind. At this level of pure planetary being, free from the tidal changes of the lunar world, solar spirit is expressed through a concerted organization of creative planetary forces - through the "universal brotherhood" of the planets.

To understand these things means very much indeed to the astrologer seeking to interpret the birth-chart of an individual. Much of the confusion found in many astrological analyses is due to the astrologer's inability to separate in his or her own mind the sphere of action of life (the realm of soli-lunar activity) from that of a man's essential individuality or identity (the realm of the planets). These two spheres obviously act and react upon each other; they interpenetrate at almost every point. Yet they refer to two basically different types of processes within the human person. To integrate these is perhaps the most important task of an individual seeking to demonstrate real maturity and integral selfhood.

The distinction between the inward and outward series of planets, with the earth as a starting point, establishes a polarization recognized in traditional Ptolemaic astrology. Mars is said to be active or masculine; Venus, receptive or feminine. Jupiter finds in Mercury its negative pole. And this principle of polarization is expressed in the planets' "rulership" over zodiacal signs, as we shall see in a subsequent chapter.

Another kind of pairing of planets brings together planets whose functions complement each other in a somewhat different manner. The couples are constituted by two successive planets in the series which originates in the Sun and spreads outward: thus Mercury and Venus, Earth and Mars, Jupiter and Saturn, Uranus and Neptune, Pluto and "X" (Proserpine?). This pairing has value particularly in a kind of heliocentric (Sun-centered) astrology in which the human intelligence seeks to understand the universe in a fully objective and "detached" manner; but it applies also to the more familiar and traditional type of astrology (geocentric or earth-centered). The two-by-two linking has significance in terms of *the work* which the planets, symbolically speaking, accomplish. Mercury and Venus are as inseparable in actual operation as electricity and magnetism; likewise Jupiter and Saturn constitute the two poles of all social activity, and Uranus and Neptune those found in all processes of metamorphosis (organic and psychological). Mars and the earth are likewise related, in the sense in which momentum and mass are related.

Still another classification of the planet divides them into planets up to and including Saturn, and trans-Saturnian planets. The first category includes all planets which, being visible to the naked eye, are matters of common, generic and biological-sensorial experience. They may be called the "planets of organic living" or "planets of the conscious" (cf. my book, *The Astrology of Personality*). The second category refers to planets discovered by means of telescopes, mathematical calculations, or photographic investigations - that is, through various products of abstract intellectual activity and engineering skill. These remote planets (Uranus, Neptune, Pluto, etc.) are thus "planets of transcendent activity" - planets symbolizing functions whose evolutionary purpose it is to make an individual greater than he normally is as a biological earth-conditioned entity. These functions act through mostly unconscious channels, through spectacular and utterly transforming visitations. They act, in *both* a constructive and a destructive manner - tearing down or dissolving the known in order to lead men to the unknown.

This type of classification is probably the most basic because it is established on the fact that every whole is part of a greater whole. For this reason two forces are operating within every whole and affecting its component parts: one of them is the gravitational pull of its center - the other is the attraction toward the "greater whole" i.e. toward the Unknown, the Transcendent. Thus Sun and Galaxy are the two poles of planetary activity. One group of planets - *which we call "planets of organic living"* - is polarized by the Sun. The other group - the *"planets of transcendent activity"* beyond Saturn's orbit - serves to link the solar world with the cosmic (and, *to us,* transcendent) realm of the "Fixed Stars". They constitute the "path" between the *natural* order of living and the state of creative emanation which we associate with the light-radiating stars; and this path is in many cases a battlefield.

I. PLANETS OF ORGANIC LIVING

These planets can be divided into three pairs, each of which has very distinct characteristics. Mercury and Venus are found inside of the earth's orbit and have no satellites. The Earth and Mars have respectively one and two satellites. Jupiter and Saturn are of giant size and accompanied by a vast number of satellites. Seen from the geocentric point of view, Mercury and Venus refer to man's "inner being". Mars releases what has reached the state of materiality and concreteness on the Earth, and through the generative power of the Moon. Jupiter and Saturn deal with the establishment of a larger "frame of reference" in which the separate earth-born entities can find their place and function, and thus can give a conscious meaning to their existence.

These six "solar planets" constitute an organic group, a structural whole through which the tide of solar activity operates incessantly. What astrologers have failed to realize is that this solar tide *has an ebb as well as a flow.* There is a circulation of solar radiation within this system of planets which can be likened to the circulation of the blood. The blood leaves the heart through the arteries, returns by way of the veins after having vivified every organ's characteristic activity. There may, or may not be, anything like arteries and veins in the solar system, but the circulation of solar radiations is undoubtedly related to the 11-year sun-spots cycle. Every planet it touches can be said to have an "arterial" and a "venous" type of activity and function. The characteristics of these functions are derived, naturally and logically, from the *place* each planet occupies in the "arterial" sequence (Mercury, Venus, Earth, Mars, Jupiter, Saturn) and in the reverse "venous" sequence (Saturn, Jupiter, Mars, Earth, Venus, Mercury).

The "arterial" or outward solar tide refers to the process of *involution;* the "venous" or inward tide, to the process of *evolution.* An *involutionary* process can be illustrated by considering how a composer's inspiration (or emotional urge to create music) takes form as a musical theme with some definite tonality; then becomes a complex harmonic and polyphonic development, later an orchestral score on paper, and finally a symphony of actual sounds performed to satisfy an actual audience. *Evolution* deals with the growth and multiplication of the organic entity, and in man with the development of consciousness, values and creative endeavors.

A. The Outward Solar Tide

We start with a release of solar activity, which is at first an undifferentiated, homogeneous "potential" of being. It is the planets' function to differentiate and spread out this solar potential, transforming it into several basic types of forces.

Mercury produces the first differentiation and the result is *electricity* - not however the type of electricity which manifests as lightning, as much as the electricity found to be the substance of all organic and cellular processes, as has been demonstrated by scientists such as Dr. Crile. Mercury's path in the sky, as seen from the earth, constitutes a kind of shuttle motion whose high points are its "inferior" and "superior" conjunctions with the Sun.

This motion symbolizes well the process of induction of electrical impulses in an alternative current.

Electricity does not operate alone. Science today has come to realize that every living organism is, at the level of operative forces, an "electro-magnetic field" - or as the occultist would say, an "astral matrix", a "web of forces". Mercury supplies the electricity, Venus is the symbol of all magnetic processes. An electrical current sent through a coil of wires (copper is the metal of Venus) induces magnetism and creates an electro-magnetic field. Such a field is a zone of influence within which particles of many substances are compelled to assume definite patterns, along the otherwise invisible "lines of forces" of the field.

Venus, receiving the solar energy after it has become transformed by Mercury into electrical current, produces a magnetic field, which releases the formative power latent in the solar outpourings. The archetypal form (or "seed form") of the organism is produced within the Venusian field (a kind of dynamic matrix, not to be confused with the lunar womb). Venus is, thus, the controlling power directing the formation of all seeds. It establishes the pattern of the oak in every acorn, the "pattern of Man" in every fecundated human ovum - and, at a higher level, the "Divine Form" (the *Augoeides* of Platonic mystics) within every human soul "impregnated" by the spirit.

With Mars, we reach the realm of organic activity directed outward. The solar tide acts now from an organic body (and at the psycho-mental level, from an ego-centered consciousness) as from a new base of operation; and the solid, dense, unyielding nature of this earthly base is such that the existence of the solar source comes to be forgotten, and the body and the ego act as *substitutes* for the creative solar spirit; Martian impulsiveness taking the place of the primordial solar "desire" for manifestation. But while the latter operates always in answer to an external need and in order to re-establish cosmic harmony and wholeness, Mars' desires are usually yearnings of the earth organism (or ego) for "self-expression" or for release of an unbearable inner pressure, regardless of what the consequences might be for those affected by the release, Mars controls, thus, all mechanisms of physical and psychological release - the muscles of the body and the personal will.

After Mars, the solar tide flowing outward meets the realm of the Asteroids, then Jupiter. Mars, being action directed outward from an established earth's center, is a conquest of space. But space is not empty. Space is filled, at best, with the remains of disintegrated worlds (the Asteroids) - remains which the Martian conqueror can subjugate - or else, with a host of entities which may challenge effectively his onward march. In the first case, a way must be found to *assimilate* the encountered remains of the past; in the second, to establish with those opposing further progress some kind of *cooperation*. These two alternatives represent the basic functions of Jupiter, in relation to the centrifugal tide of solar activity. Jupiter, in the body, refers to all processes of food-assimilation (liver, pancreas, duodenum, etc.) At the level of collective human living, Jupiter expands the individual's sphere of personal activity by relating it to those of other men's endeavor. Relationship leads to the "feel" of group-cooperation, to an increase of power, thus to a sense of greater living and success. Social life is born as a result, and the realization that one belongs to a larger whole, that one can use the power of this larger whole when needed.

The next step is to make this sense of communal being and of personal intensification through group-relationship *more permanent*. This is the task of Saturn. Saturn builds all conceivable types of social or group structures - any structure, that is, which defines the "place" which an individual occupies in a group. At a mental level, Saturn manifests as the power of rigorous, logical thinking which certifies the right that any idea or statement has to precede or follow other ideas or statements.

Saturn makes the individual's place in the greater whole not only well defined, but unchallengeable and secure. It guarantees to any man that he will remain what he is; and this means actually that he will maintain his place, basic characteristics and position against the pressure of change, and especially against the intrusion of individuals more powerful than he is as a single person. Saturn guarantees him that he is not, in fact, a single, solitary person. The power of the whole community - of its laws and its police force - is back of him ... provided he remains in the place where he belongs. At the organic level, Saturn represents the skeleton, because it is the function of the skeleton to keep every organ where it belongs in relation to the "law" of the human organism.

With Saturn we reach the sun's polar opposite. The sun is a well-spring of constant outpourings of light and life-potential. It is pure creativeness. Saturn is just the opposite: it sets every type of differentiated activity in a definite, unmodifiable place. It is pure stability - negatively, absolute rigidity. Nevertheless Saturn fulfills the purpose of the Sun; for each solar release, if considered as an individual source of life-processes, aims at fulfilling the need for integration of a certain type of material particles (or of chaotic psychic remains). True integration not only requires a Venusian archetype defining the solar pattern of organic integration, and a concrete organism generated within the lunar womb; it also demands that the organism be able to express its integrated self (or natural being), for it is only through "expression" that a man becomes *aware* of himself, whether as the result of enmity or of group-cooperation.

This awareness is greatest as the individual comes to know his place in a larger social whole. Knowing his place and function in this whole he also knows how others know him. "Con-sciousness" means literally "knowing together". There can only be consciousness for man, as man knows how other men - his peers or superiors, or even his inferiors - know him. Consciousness is the outcome of shared awareness, of awareness of self answering to and probing into the awareness of others. Saturn defines the foundation of consciousness (and as well of individual selfhood) *by placing it within a stable frame of reference.* Saturn turns negative and an obstacle to human growth only when the need for stability becomes a yearning for security at any cost. Then the Saturnian frame of reference becomes a prison; clear and logical thinking becomes dogma; selfhood becomes a shell; the ego, a tyrant.

B. *The Inward Tide*

Consciousness rises from the Saturnian foundation and reaches back toward the Sun. This is the ebb of life. The living organism and the living ego, now established in structural stability, experience the unfoldment of their individual powers. They experience organic growth.

To be conscious of one's rightful and permanent place and function in one's group, one's nation, one's race - and ultimately in humanity as a persistent organic whole - and to feel the stability of it beyond any doubt means to have realized that one is an individual self. The more unique this position, the sharper the sense of individual selfhood. As a "personal ego" man is still insecure and ephemeral. As a genius, whose fame remains through centuries, the individual acquires social immortality - thus a collective permanency. As a "spiritual Identity" whose consciousness endures beyond death, the individual reaches the goal of cyclic immortality, retaining his "place" through an entire cycle of humanity's development. At every step, man says "I"; but saying it means more and more. It means greater integration and a more total fulfillment of the original solar purpose.

To know one's selfhood is not enough. This knowledge would be empty if not vivified by the feeling of one's constant participation in the life of one's community, and eventually of humanity or of the universe. It would be meaningless if the other members of the group were not warmly responsive to this participation. And here Jupiter comes in, transfiguring ego into soul, social cooperation into religious communion, individual selfhood into the mystic experience of unity which men call God. The consciousness of the Saturnian "I" becomes ever more *inclusive and significant;* and Jupiter pours into the return tide of solar power the ferment of compassion and understanding. The greater the inclusiveness of the unit, the more the life of the whole seeks to manifest through the unit's activity. The individual becomes a representative man, endowed with "authority".

On the basis of whatever degree of Jupiterian inclusiveness an individual consciously operates, the Mars function then acts as a drive toward the solar spirit. Mars is then the power of devotion and of self-sacrifice - and negatively of fanaticism. It is faith; and faith is always based on a sense of inner assurance (Saturn) and on a feeling of participation with others or with the universe (Jupiter).

In the realm of the Earth "faith" leads to "works". The Earth is not considered as a planet in geocentric astrology; but, in its stead, the Moon - especially when at Full Moon, *outside* of the earth's orbit - gathers in the substance of the outer planets' inward strivings and *generates* with it "organisms of consciousness". She is then the Muse, the inspiring woman, the servant of the gods. She brings to man's consciousness Images of spiritual activity - and as she performs this task, she is the *anima* of Jungian psychology. Indeed she reflects even what has happened beyond Saturn's boundaries.

The ebbing solar tide then reaches the realm of Venus; and in this realm everything comes to bloom. It is the realm of beauty and of conscious love, because it is, above all, the realm of *value*. Culture and art are born from this sense of "value" - and likewise morality and the highest quality of sharing which illumines the return of consciousness to its solar source. Venus is still "magnetism"; but, in terms of consciousness, this means "love", and true love is the feeling which emerges from the individual's sharing in objects of value, in ideals and in cultural group-images. Such a sharing establishes *community* patterns polarizing the *organic* patterns which Venus had built at the corresponding level of the outward tide of solar activity.

Mercury generalizes the values to which Venus gives form into concepts and abstractions. Mercury is memory and the faculty of mental association. It is the granary in which every factor of life in its seed state receives a clear and expressible meaning. What was structure (Saturn), feeling of participation (Jupiter), faith (Mars) and value (Venus) reaches now the final stage of growth as thought. Images become ideas; and ideas - like seeds - can be transferred. They can be carried to all men, in space and time, by language and words. They are the seed of immortal being - the journey's end.

The solar tide returns to the heart of the Sun having done its work; having given *life* to the planetary spheres and received from them *meaning*. What was *power* in the beginning has become in the end *consciousness*. *From* consciousness a new tide of creative power surges forth out of the inexhaustible heart of the Sun, and the process is renewed at a higher level - if all has been well with the previous tide!

2. PLANETS OF TRANSCENDENT ACTIVITY

The greatness of man is that he can always be greater. This urge to be greater, this incessant reaching out for vaster horizons and for the beyond of the known, is latent in every individual. It beats upon the consciousness or the feelings of men who are more daring or more restless, more evolved or more abnormal. It seizes them with a passion for transcendence and a rebelliousness against all traditions and limitations. It axes at the set Saturnian "frames of reference" with an insistence from which anger and fury are not always absent.

This will to metamorphosis is expressed in astrology by the remote planets Uranus and Neptune. Together with Pluto, these constitute what we are able to know, today, of the still mysterious realm which links the solar system (as seen from the Earth) with the cosmic world of the Galaxy, the "Universal Brotherhood of Stars". These three remote planets refer to an intermediary realm and to a process of transition. In terms of individual experience and consciousness, they define the nature of the "path" which (according to mystics and occultists of all ages) a man must tread in order to become more-than-human - that is, an expression of the divine in a human form.

These planets are seemingly parts of the solar system; yet they actually are attached to it more than they "belong" to it. In a very real sense, they are ambassadors from, and representatives of, the Galaxy. They are here, in the solar realm, to perform a definite job: the job of showing to whomever seeks to rise beyond the pull of the solar tide *the way out and beyond.*

Uranus clears up the path that leads through the Saturnian boundaries. Neptune dissolves every personal feeling that clings still to the adventurer into the beyond. Pluto produces a new pattern of integration with an insistence that tends to obliterate even the memory of the past, pulverizing the structures of old and cementing the remains into a screen upon which to project the new Image. Uranus is the inspirer of revolt, the lightning that reveals for a brief blinding moment the vistas hidden by our very demand for security and rightful ownership. Such moments can transform all the implications of existence. Neptune, on the contrary, is the slow-working "universal solvent" which attacks the substance of customary living and of ego-centered consciousness. It forces the particular to fade out into the universal; and as this happens strange and fantastic illusions and mirages are likely to appear.

Yet these planets destroy only in order to renew. They are planets of metamorphosis. They bring to the realm of the solar planets and to earth-born individuals a breath of the Stars. And that breath is filled with creative powers of a transcendent character. These, however, cannot take root in man, unless man's nature is free from the *negative* characteristics of Mars, Jupiter and Saturn - lust or anger, greed and selfishness.

Uranus and Neptune have been called "higher octaves" of Mercury and Venus. What should be said, rather, is that man can receive the constructive gifts of Uranus and Neptunes *only* when the forces represented by Mercury and Venus have been allowed to operate fully *on the return solar tide.* These forces alone can pro-

vide a foundation for the development of "star-ward" consciousness under the guidance of Uranus and Neptune. Neptune needs
the Venusian sense of value and of sharing in love in order to
build the "concrete universals" (the inclusive and compassionate
structures) which are the transcendent vehicles of expression of
the universal spirit; and Uranus can bring clear visions of the star-
world only to him who has a strong and steady capacity to think
in terms of ideas and abstractions (Mercury).

As to Pluto, it seems probable that this newly discovered planet
is only the first of a pair or trinity of very distant and comet-like
planets, probably with very elongated orbits. Such planets refer
to the process of reconstruction at the end of the metamorphosis,
to the action of groups, even more than of individuals. Pluto deals
with the "style" of an art period, rather than with the characteristics of the individual artists. It reveals the impact of civilization
upon the genesis of individuals. If it refers to death, it is because
it has no regard for individuals and it is ready to destroy any organism in order to use its physical and psychic substances for new
purposes. Pluto is the impersonal discipline of the Party, the
Church, the Brotherhood. Only through its ordeals is the reborn
individual "trans-substantiated" enough to become incorporated
into the fabric of the universal organism which emerged from the
strange matrix of Neptunian test-tubes.

THE SEVENTH STEP

Acquiring a Sense of Form and Accentuation

In the first stage of this study I defined the term, structure, as the result of the workings of the principle of organization within any organic whole. I spoke of the "web of relationships" established within the boundaries of this whole and determining the place which every part occupies in relation to every other part. Form, in the general and abstract sense of the word, has almost the same meaning as structure; but it applies more specifically to the result of the perception by an individual of the wholeness of the whole. A picture and a body "have form" as we see them in their entirety. Form can thus be considered as the outer manifestation of internal structure. The sense of form is the ability to see objects and bodies as structured wholes, to see them as balanced and proportioned entities spread out in space.

The sense of form is found in its highest and most significant aspect in the artist - painter, sculptor, architect. To him space is in itself a womb of significant forms. Every object in space has meaning in terms of its relationship to every other object. Every time he opens his eyes, the world that the artist perceives is an organic and significant aggregation of forms. These forms interpenetrate, in as much as they react upon each other within the range of the field of vision. Not only colors, lights and shades cast reflections from object to object, but even the structural masses of these objects cannot be considered as isolated or separate.

As some European painters were able to discover some sixty years ago, if a man is seen sitting on a sofa, the man and the sofa

interact and interpenetrate - that is to say, the forms of the two
react upon each other as they are perceived together as a composite whole. Even more so, bits of colors in a painting acquire
special characteristics and esthetic meaning according to their relative placing within the space of the canvas. A red dash in a green
landscape stands out with exaggerated intensity; it focuses inevitably the attention of the eye; and painters, like Corot, make constant use of such color juxtapositions to express drama, or simply
to emphasize structural values, distortions, etc.

In recent years this principle of form-awareness has become the
subject of a very keen and detailed type of psychological observation. The German school of *Gestalt* psychology is based on the
study of the factor of form in human perceptions. *Gestalt* means
form, structure or spatial organization.

To the psychologist devoted to this type of psychological approach the sense of form appears as one of the most basic elements in human perception, and as an equally characteristic factor
in the development of individual personality. Individuals can be
classified according to their typical response to associational patterns of dots, lines, spaces, and objects. The phenomena of optical
illusions, featured recently in op art are applications of this inquiry
into the nature of our sense of form. They simply emphasize what
occurs to some extent every time we open our eyes and see objects
in space.

"Form" in Astrology

As man is born at a point of the earth's surface, he finds himself surrounded not only by earthly objects but by the infinity of
celestial bodies moving in space. The birth-chart is a two-dimensional projection of the universe - and particularly of our solar system and its planets - as seen from the place of birth at the time of
the first breath ... or rather, as it would be seen if we could see
through the solid globe of the earth! What this birth-chart features is the Sun, the Moon and the planets. They are objects arran-
ged in space (the space of the sky itself, and the space defined by

the circle of yearly motion of the Sun, viz. the zodiac). At night, some of these planets can be seen above the horizon, others are invisible. But by looking at the astrological chart we can visualize their positions all around us. If one of these celestial bodies is alone above the horizon, and all the rest below, anybody's sense of form should be developed enough to become aware of this peculiar balancing of objects. The object which finds itself alone is singled out by the eyes, and the attention is as focused upon it as when a red dot appears in a completely green landscape.

There is a focusing of attention, however, only as long as the chart is considered *as a whole* - or let us say, as a picture or scene. Until recently such a way of looking at a chart was practically unknown among astrologers. It is true that "aspects" between planets were studied - and these are the expressions of space-relationship between celestial objects. But these angular patterns were studied one by one. Earlier still, the use of a square-shaped astrological chart made it very difficult to "see" the chart as a whole, as an image of the actual universe. Each planet stood as a unit, and its nature remained always the same - it being merely *modified* by the place it occupied in the zodiacal and house spaces, and by the "rays" of other planets according to their "aspects" to it. Indeed there was little sense in erecting a chart at all; a simple listing of planetary positions and aspects told all that was to be known.

The definite use of the circular chart, however, led logically to the realization that the element of form or *gestalt* was essential in astrology. Astrologers began to talk of the "planetary pattern" as a whole and to give meaning to it *independently* of which planet was in aspect to which. It was Marc Edmund Jones' perhaps most important contribution to astrology to build upon this principle of form, first, by stressing the concept of "balance in weight" and "singleton" influence - then, later, by classifying charts according to the over-all shape produced by the disposition of the planets in the circle of houses, and secondarily in the zodiac.*

* Another type of astrological technique which features in a somewhat different way the sense of form and the configurational or even pictorial approach to the

One may or may not consider as essential Marc Jones' classification of over-all planetary patterns into seven basic patterns; one may or may not consider the names given to these seven types significant. The fact remains that a *principle of astrological evaluation and meaning* has been stated and developed with logical consistency and this is eminently significant. Indeed this fact can no longer be ignored by anyone who is attuned to the fundamentals of twentieth century thinking. The sense of astrological form is with us to stay; and its practical use is indispensable to the full attainment of "astrological wisdom". All that can really be discussed is its relative importance among the other and more traditional tools used by the astrologer in its interpretations.

The problem can be stated as follows: Is it better to teach the child to read by making him recognize at first the shape of syllables or words, or by the old method of laboriously spelling letter after letter? Is sense (or significance) to be taught as the result of an addition of separate, abstract and in themselves meaningless elements (letters) - or, in the new way, through a quick perception of a few typical but complex patterns which in themselves have associative meaning? The little bird learns to fly by being made to visualize a scene enacted by its parents. All instinctual guidance is guidance through imitative performance; all biological development is by whole-steps - by *quanta* of behavior, one might say.

There is no real growth in life-efficiency except by facing at any time a *situation as a whole* with the whole of one's ability to survive; likewise there is no real growth in human understanding and in wisdom except the growing individual is made to meet the challenge of total and particular situations, situations which are unique and significant in their uniqueness. What the modern mind is forced to deal with today are situations, facts of living immediacy and urgency, wholes of behavior, complete symbols of a total

study of the birth-chart is the so-called "Uranian System" developed by Alfred Witte and his Hamburg School in Germany. A good deal of attention has been given to it of late in America and a number of points which it brings out are undoubtedly of great significance, especially the "mid-points".

personality, rather than lists of characteristics, sum-totals of cata-
logued traits and nicely defined virtues or faults, and the pasting
together of abstract judgments in the conventionalized shape of a
human personality!

Jupiter-in-Leo, Sun-in-the-third-house, Mars-square-Saturn mean
nothing *final* in themselves. They are at best the raw materials
from which *vital meanings* can be moulded by the perceptive effort and the visualizing "intuitive" skill of the astrologer. The letters L, O, V, E spelt one after the other mean nothing as separate
letters; it is their association and the order of their sequence which
release significance. No astrological chart, likewise, makes sense
until it is a living whole in the consciousness of the astrologer -
until its "form" has become in-spirited with meaning. And the
meaning resides in the whole, not in the separate parts.

The Problem of Accentuation

Almost inseparable from the concept of form is that of "accent". Whenever a number of organic factors are related within
the boundaries of an organism, there is at any time some one factor (or group of factors) which, in one way or another, has a dominant or leading function. It is accentuated. And this accentuation, in any healthy organism, is only temporary. It shifts from one
factor to another, from one organic function to another; and the
shifting is in most cases, or should be, periodical. If we consider
the cycle of vegetation throughout the year we can see readily
how, month after month, there is a shift in the function which receives, as it were, the spotlight in the plant's development. At one
time, life seems focused in the rootlet or germ; at another, the
development of leaves seems to draw most of the plant's energies;
still at another period flowers and fruits carry the burden of significance, the temporary life-emphasis or accent.

Likewise after a hearty dinner the metabolic activities of the
digestive system are the accentuated functions in the total human
organism; and if, at such times, the individual with a full stomach
indulges in heavy mental work, an organic conflict between two

types of functions arises. One accent wars against the other - thought against metabolism, and *vice versa*. Normal and natural health requires that there be only one accentuated function in the bio-psychological organism of the personality at any time. Thus, the concept of a *permutation of functional accents* arises; which simply means that each function, in turn and periodically, is to receive the life-accent.

This is expressed in astrology, first of all, in the factors of zodiacal or house position. If the Sun is in Cancer, we can deduce that the organic functions represented by Cancer (metabolism, assimilation, home-making, ego-building) are shown to receive at the time the *solar accent*. This does not mean that the other eleven basic or zodiacal functions are not active. It merely indicates that the attention of the self is focused upon the Cancerian function. Other functions are at the same time particularly energized by the other planets. Jupiter in Leo will show that social consciousness (Jupiter) seeks to release its energy *mainly* through the imaginative and creative Leo function and its corresponding organs - biological or psychological.

Every sign of the zodiac or every house in which a planet is located receives thereby an accent. It is emphasized in the life of the personality. And these accents are constantly and cyclically changing, as the planets, Sun and Moon revolve through our skies. Yet these are, in a sense, lesser accents. Stronger accents are established, according to astrological tradition, when the moving celestial bodies are found in one or two particular zodiacal signs. And these strong accents refer to what is technically called "rulership" or "exaltation". Each planet is said to "rule" one or two signs of the zodiac, and to be "exalted" in another; however, much confusion surrounds such a subject, the study of which would require too much space. By means of technical procedures of this type the astrologer is able to ascertain the relative "strength" of every planet in a chart - thus the degree to which some basic functions of the total personality are accentuated, or, in the opposite signs, weak in their operations.

Such a type of accentuation, however, is not an emphasis in consciousness as much as one in potential activity. The Sun in Leo is very "strong", yet a person born with the Sun in Leo may not reveal any corresponding solar accent. The astrologer will say that the Son may be "weak" by house position - some houses supposedly representing weaker zones of function - even while it is "strong" because of being located in its sign of rulership, Leo. However, the attribution of characteristics of weakness or strength to houses is very questionable. It makes sense only if one takes for granted that *external* activity is the criterium; for there are hidden or introverted factors in the human person which acquire an extraordinary focal significance, and which rule the life by the very absence of their natural activities. They are accentuated, not by what they do, but by the void they create in a person's consciousness. There are accents in emptiness, as well as in fullness - in critical change (for instance, the sixth house) as well as in positive self-assertion (first or tenth house).

More than this, the real problem of life-accent depends not upon where any planet is, but rather upon the type of relationship it has to the remainder of the planets. The red dot in the green landscape is a tiny little spot of color; but how it draws the attention, how it focuses the dramatic meaning of the entire painting! It is an accent which gives a new kind of intensity to all that is not itself. It makes the picture far more green than if it had not been there.

A "singleton" planet in a chart has much the same value. This single planet accentuates the function it represents *in the consciousness of the individual* - and perhaps, as a result, in his contribution to life - to such an extent that the individual cannot let go of it. Indeed this accentuation or focusing of attention has very often a compulsive character. Everything else is affected by it.

Characteristic is the case of Freud, founder of the psycho-analytical method, in whose chart Mars retrograde stands alone at the nadir in Libra, with all other planets above the horizon, from Pisces to Cancer (Cancer being the rising sign). According to his

81

one-time disciple, Carl Jung, Freud's approach to psychology reveals a typical extrovert temperament - which is represented by
the fact that most planets are bunched around the zenith, especially in the three spring signs, etc. Yet in Freud's field of consciousness, driving him to his great achievements, we find Mars
retrograde cutting like a scalpel into the innermost roots of his
inner life, cutting away the decaying psychic materials produced by
social repressions. His whole life was devoted to, and his name
became the symbol of this introverted Martian soul-surgery - of
that which is most intimately personal, and hidden even to the ego
itself.

Here, then, Mars is an intensely accentuated factor in terms of
the "form" of the entire chart; yet, according to its zodiacal position and its retrograde character, it might appear (if considered as
a separate factor) a very weak and ineffective Mars. The astrologer who fails to exercise his "sense of form" will miss in his interpretation of Freud's chart that element which controls, by implication, the behavior of everything else in the nativity. Freud's life
and fame showed forth an extraordinary one-pointedness and a
ruthless challenge to the most established psychological traditions.
Nothing can reveal in their proper value these outstanding features except the over-all pattern of the chart and the Mars accent.
The structural relationship between Mars and the nine other planets, bunched within a square of Neptune and Jupiter to Saturn, is
the key to the meaning of Freud's destiny.

Such a type of approach when properly understood and applied,
gives a new and very vital quality to the interpretation of astrological charts. It should be clear that this approach is based on the
fundamental principle that *the whole is prior to the parts* in terms
of essential, spiritual meaning. This principle actually differentiates wisdom from knowledge, the spiritual faculties of understanding from the intellect, the astrology of the twentieth century
from that of the nineteenth.

THE EIGHTH STEP

A Dynamic Understanding of Planetary Cycles and Aspects

The preceding step in the development of an attitude toward astrology and of a technique leading to a vital understanding of human life and personality dealt with the acquisition of a sense of form and accentuation. The term "form" however includes far more than I have been considering so far. What I discussed is primarily form *in space,* thus, form as a static element, as something which can be apprehended in a single act of perception - for instance, the form of a painting, of the decorative pattern of a rug. If we look at a modern astrological chart we can see at once its circular pattern, its twelve spokes, the symbols of the planets, the zodiacal indications, etc. And the point which I made was that the essential significance of a nativity (of the pattern of the sky at birth) can only be grasped when the astrologer is able to consider and interpret the chart as a structural and "organic" whole. First, the perception of the whole; then, the analytical study of the parts and of the details of the structure.

Form, however, can be considered also as a dynamic factor, operating *in time;* that is, in terms of cyclic sequence. It is so considered, for instance, by trained musicians when they speak of the "sonata-form" or of the structural design of a Bach "fugue". A sonata and a fugue cannot be experienced through one single act of perception. You cannot hear them or even look at the scores and realize the structural meaning in the same way in which you look at a drawing. They spread out in time; it takes time for the musician to perceive the "form" of the sonata as he listens to it

83

from beginning to end - even if he is able to read quickly the pages of the printed score.

Likewise it takes time for the astrologer to go through the pages of ephemeris and to follow day by day, month by month, the zodiacal movements of the planets. The ephemeris reveals the principle of "form" in operation as well as a Beethoven sonata does. It does so because the motions of the Sun, the Moon and the planets are periodical or cyclic. And the constant combination of these cyclic motions - the ceaseless interweaving of the planets' paths in the sky - produce *dynamic forms.*

This being understood, I will consider what is called a "square" aspect of Jupiter and Saturn - that is, the fact that their zodiacal longitudes are 90 degrees apart. The first point to deal with, however, is one that astrologers who talk about the significance of a square fail to consider. I said I am considering a square; but *where* am I considering it? In the birth-chart of an individual, or in the ephemeris?

The reader may exclaim here: Is it not the same square in either case? It is the same square if we take Jupiter and Saturn out of the contexts in which we find them (the birth-chart or the ephemeris); if we separate them from everything else that surrounds them, and thus if we make of them purely abstract entities. But actually the square has two different meanings according to whether it is perceived in the birth-chart - a *spatial and static* structure - or in the ephemeris - a *dynamic time* structure. You look at a chart all at once. You read the ephemeris line by line, page by page. The chart represents a fixed event, which is unalterable - you (as a personal organism) are born only once and you will never get a new birth-chart. On the other hand, the ephemeris records a constantly unrolling sequence of events, and the "forms" it reveals are the results of the regular and cyclic way in which celestial bodies move.

Thus a Jupiter-Saturn square analyzed in a birthchart is a static, spatial factor; but the same square considered in the pages of an ephemeris is a dynamic, time factor. In the first case it belongs to something that is set once and for all; in the second case, it is a factor which will recur periodically throughout the ages. In the birth-chart the Jupiter-Saturn square is a part of the entire structure of the chart *and must be understood as such;* while in the ephemeris it is part of the cyclic interweavings of the two moving planets, Jupiter and Saturn, and must therefore be understood *with reference to these planets' cyclic interweavings.*

To sum up: If a student asks me: "Mr. X has a square of Jupiter and Saturn in his birth-chart. What does it mean?" I shall answer: "I cannot answer your question unless I study the chart as a whole and the place which the Jupiter and Saturn relation occupies in it." But if the student asks: "What does the square of Jupiter in Leo 10° to Saturn in Scorpio 10° mean?" - then, I can answer directly; for here the question deals with the relationship between Jupiter and Saturn considered in one of its periodically repeated *phases.*

Planetary Aspects as Phases of Relationships

It is rather difficult for most people to think in terms of actually unfolding time and of relatedness. Through the centuries of a civilization stressing an intellectual approach to life, we have been used to thinking of separate and permanent entities located in very definite and distinct places in a static space. These entities might change completely in appearance; yet we have thought of them in the past as having an abstract integrity, an unalterable identity. Whether young, mature or senile - whether they are found relatively alone or deeply involved in relationship with other entities - they have been given distinct names and we have thought that they remain essentially what they were.

This "classical" type of mental understanding of life and men has been gradually changing in the present century. And the pressure of that change is compelling astrologers to reorient and reinterpret their own essential ideas and symbols. Astrological textbooks tend to speak of Jupiter and Saturn - and of all the other factors they use - as if they were set entities meaning always the same thing whenever found. Likewise squares, trines, oppositions are taught to have a generally unchanging significance: indeed both planets and aspects have been divided for ages into two categories: "bad" ones and "good" ones - benefics and malefics.

To do so, obviously simplifies things a great deal. It produces in front of us a very clear-cut, black and white universe in which good and evil fight ceaselessly for control over separate entities which are individually saved or lost, glorified or destroyed. Contemporary thinking, however, challenges this "old time" philosophy of life and its atomistic individualism. The universe is now seen as an interconnected and interdependent whole - an organism of cosmic scope. And the basic reality of this universe is not the separate entity going to its salvation or its doom, but instead the total inter-relatedness of all the parts composing the cosmic whole.

This means, in terms of astrology, that the interrelatedness of all the celestial bodies within the solar system (and in general in the whole sky) is what essentially counts, and that any one of these bodies *can, under special conditions of relationship, mean practically anything* - in particular, it can have a significance exactly opposed to its traditionally accepted one. Likewise the finest human individual can, under the stress of special types of relationship, turn highly destructive *in his actions*. This has been stated by saying that everything tends to become its opposite. It is, however, an over-simplified statement; for the point is not that an "entity" becomes the opposite of what it is, but rather that a "relationship" tends to reverse its polarity - for instance, love turns into hate, sensual passion turns into mystical devotion, etc.

It is on the basis of such an understanding of life and universal relatedness that the new astrology is reformulating the concept of planetary aspect. It sees the above-mentioned square of Jupiter to Saturn not as a thing-in-itself, but rather as a phase of the cyclic relationship of Jupiter to Saturn. The fact that the two planets are 90-degrees apart does not say enough to be considered completely significant. What is significant is that a *particular cycle* of relationship between Jupiter and Saturn has reached a *partiular phase* in its development.

As I have shown in my book THE LUNATION CYCLE, the meaning of a "waxing square" and that of a "waning square" are different; that is, if Jupiter (the faster moving planet) is in Leo 10°, and Saturn in Scorpio 10°, the square they form is a waning square (similar to a "last quarter" square in the cycle of the Moon to Sun relationship, the lunation cycle); but if the slower Saturn is in Leo 10° and Jupiter is in Scorpio 10°, then their square is a waxing (or first quarter) square. In other words, a cycle of relationship between Jupiter and Saturn begins with their conjunction and climaxes in their opposition. *Any phase of this cycle* - that is, any aspect which Jupiter and Saturn form during the period from one conjunction to the next - must be understood within the frame of reference of the entire cycle. Eventually, in a more inclusive study, it would have to be understood also within the still larger frame of reference of the vast cycle of planetary interrelationship involving all the components of the solar system.

It is evident that this gives to the astrological theory a more complex character than that displayed in most current textbooks. Likewise Einstein's physics is far more complex than Newton's. If we wish to deal with physical events obvious to our senses Newton's laws work very satisfactorily; and the classical astrology which dealt with set meanings for set planetary positions and aspects (and with innumerable aphorisms to be memorized) also worked well in relation to the type of society in which seventeenth century persons were living. But we have today a far different world confronting us, a world of atomic energy and of vast metropoles, of cartels and global interchanges, with social and personal relationships so complex and so fluid that great quantities of individuals are caught in social difficulties and in psychological conditions with which old techniques cannot deal effectively. For this kind of a world we need astrology, as much as physicists needed a new algebra and a new physics to control atomic transformations and disintegrations - even though the classical concepts of

87

physics and astrology are still most useful where standard situations and problems are concerned.

Good and Bad Aspects

Typical among the traditional concepts of astrology which need to be reinterpreted or revised today is the idea that aspects such as squares and oppositions are "bad", while trines and sextiles are "good". Such a belief is obviously meaningless in the type of astrology I am discussing in this book; for squares are as much *normal and necessary phases* in the cyclic relationship between two moving planets as are trines or sextiles. Evil - as normally understood by the average person - ceases to have meaning if it can be shown that it is as normal and necessary as good.

We say that the disease, cancer, is an evil; and the statement is valid because cancer is neither normal nor necessary. But if we say that the breakdown into chemical substances of the food we eat is an evil process because it destroys the carrot or the calf liver into an amorphous pulp, or if we say that the replacement of worn out cells in our body by new ones is "bad" - such assertions have no valid meaning. Every phase of normal organic living, every function and process which is part of natural, healthy living - physiologically or psychologically - is to be welcomed. It is neither good nor bad. It simply *is* - a necessary component of the activities of life or of personality. There is in every organism a dynamic balance between anabolic (or form building) and catabolic (or form liquidating) processes; but to call the former good and the latter bad makes no sense at all. The exaggerated and unchecked development of either type is destructive of normal organic life, of the health of body and soul.

It is true that the progressive increase of catabolic activities with age leads eventually to death; but it is highly questionable whether saying that natural death is bad has any valid meaning. Certainly, from the point of view of mankind as a whole, the death of human beings is a condition necessary for evolutionary growth, considering the psycho-mental level at which the average human consciousness functions today. The character of an individual and the limits of his possible development are usually well set in his twenties or thirties. If it remained set for centuries it would indeed be a tragedy for humanity!

The death-process represents for mankind as a whole what the catabolic process of periodical clearing up of obsolete cells means for a healthy organism. It has been said that all the cells of our body are renewed every seven years. Likewise an entire wave of individuals lasts a theoretical period of about seventy years. The catabolic replacement of one generation by another is neither good nor bad; it is the law of collective human development and growth. And if we think in terms of an absolute kind of spiritual individualism, the coming into and the coming out of the body (birth and death) are merely normal and necessary phases of the cyclic development of the reincarnating spirit.

The qualifications of good and bad have no meaning wherever they are applied to any such phases of a cyclic process; and, from a transcendent and universalistic point of view, *any event* can be seen as a necessary phase of some larger process. A pneumonia may be called bad because it is not a normal phase of our body's life; wars and political purges are bad because they are not normal phases of the social life of a particular community. Nevertheless, considered within the larger frame of reference of a spiritual soul's progress (incarnation after incarnation) or of humanity as a whole, these destructive events may appear as necessary and beneficent as the forceful ejection from the body of substances which cannot be assimilated. It is only if we isolate the social or personal cathartic event from the total history of nations or individuals - and the square, semi-square or opposition aspects from the cycles of relationship of the planets - that these events and aspects, considered in themselves, look evil or unfortunate.

Such a procedure destroys the very integrity and meaning of the life-process. Life and personality are characterized by their capacity for constant adjustment to new internal needs and new external situations. To say that the square and opposition are bad aspects is to deny this possibility of readjustment, because readjustment necessitates always moments of rapid action (changing of gears) when a new situation or a new possibility is met "squarely", and moments of pause (opposition) when the consciousness finds itself able to evaluate objectively and dispassionately the purpose and meaning of action. Under square phases of relationship there may be much grinding of gears, and uncoordinated haste or spasmodic fear generated between the two poles of the relationship; but, to state the possibility of such negative results is not to describe the essential meaning of the square, it is to show *how an inexperienced individual spirit or an immature social group may mishandle the special type of opportunity for growth represented by the square.*

Impartiality compels me to admit that, as most individuals and nations are as yet immature and awkward engineers of their destiny, the square does produce in most cases negative results. But can I berate the gears of an excellent Chrysler car, just because a poor driver makes them grind their teeth at each change of gears? And can one say that stopping to look at a map in order to check on one's direction is bad just because a confused driver may stop in the middle of a turn in the road and, absorbed in reading the map, find himself hit by oncoming cars?

From this discussion it follows that any planetary aspect can be regarded in two ways. From the point of view of *time,* it is a phase of the cycle of relationship between two moving planets, and a thorough grasp of its significance requires that it be considered in its relation to the entire cycle - and particularly to the beginning of the cycle, the conjunction of the two planets. Thus, astrologers have often considered as basically important the zodiacal location of the new moon preceding birth - thereby referring the soli-lunar relationship at birth (i.e. the aspect between the natal Sun and Moon) to the beginning of the lunation cycle of which it was a phase.

On the other hand, from the point of view of *space,* an aspect between two planets is merely one angle of the total planetary pattern displayed by the sky at birth. And just as the shape of the nose acquires esthetic meaning mostly in what it contributes to the particular character of a beautiful face - even though, as a nose, it has in itself some general significance - likewise the aspect cannot be truly and significantly understood or interpreted unless it is seen as contributing to the picture which the chart as a whole presents.

In the first instance, the distinction between good and bad aspects makes no sense because both are necessary and normal phases of the process of life and growth - phases gradually and periodically merging into one another. In the second instance, such an opposition should be considered as analogical to that between whites and blacks in a photograph, between lights and shades in a Rembrandt painting. Would there be any meaning in saying that the blacks are evil and the whites good? Form is the result of the juxtaposition and interaction of both. And without form there can be no significant relationship and no meaning.

THE NINTH STEP

Establishing a Proper Attitude Toward Astrological Predictions

One of the most essential things to learn, as one undertakes the study of astrology, is the nature of the distinction between the two fundamental phases of astrological technique: the *spatial* phase, which refers to the study of the birth-chart (or of any set celestial pattern), and the *durational* phase, which deals with the related and periodical motions of celestial bodies through days, months and years - motions which are recorded in the tables of the ephemeris. We have studied the meaning of this distinction mainly with reference to planetary aspects and their traditional classification into good and bad categories. I stated that what is called form or structure can be considered either as a space factor, or as a time factor. The structure of a birth-chart is a space factor; that is, a combination of shapes - or more precisely of angular relationships (aspects). The chart as a whole has form, much as a painting or a statue has form. On the other hand, the columns of an ephemeris reveal another kind of form, similar to that defined in music under the name "sonata form", "fugue", etc. - form produced by cyclic sequence and development, by repetition and rhythmic accents.

The modern astrologer follows ordinarily three basic types of procedure. First, he studies the birth-chart as a combination (or sum-total) of static and set planetary and cuspal position within the frame of reference of the zodiac. Then, he enters the realm of duration and time-sequence; and the studies what are called "progressions" (or "directions") and "transits". Some astrologers

92

lay more stress on the former, others on the latter. In most cases both factors are calculated and given significance. It is usually from a study of progressions and transits that indications as to the future of the person whose birth-chart is being studied (the "native") are mostly derived; but many inferences as to future events - in terms of basic crises of growth - can also be made from the birth-chart considered as the unchanging "blueprints" of the person's character and so-called destiny.

In the next chapter I shall discuss the precise meaning of transits and progressions, and their practical fields of application. But before we come to these more specific subjects it seems imperative for me to discuss the general matter of astrological prediction and the psychological attitude held toward such predictions. It is particularly important for the would-be astrologer to realize that the moment he enters the realm of duration and of processes of growth - the realm of evolving and dynamic factors in actual experience - he is confronted with problems which differ basically from those he meets while interpreting the once-for-all set birth-pattern. Philosophers might say that the latter deals with the factor of "being", the former with "becoming" - yet these metaphysical terms may be more confusing than helpful.

It would seem best to say that the birth-chart (a space factor) refers to the *abstract character* of being, while the transits and progressions (time factors) refer to the *progressive realization* of being. To study a birth-chart is to study the "anatomy" of personality - that is, at the physical level, the place which bones, muscles and organs occupy in relation to each other and within the boundaries of the organic whole, the body. On the other hand, the progressions refer essentially to the "physiology" and "pathology" of personality, that is, to the actual functioning of organs - or more accurately, to the series of modifications brought by the process of living and of personal growth to the functions of the total organism of personality.

The anatomy of a person determines the physical (and to a large extent, the psychological) *potentialities* of life and character for this person. But what is determined is only a sum-total of "potentialities" - not actual facts or events. A weak or twisted body may become either the structural foundation for a brilliant, successful individual, or the curse of a hopeless personality. Acute psychological complexes can serve the goal of self-realization or lead to fruitless neurosis.

When the astrologer interprets the birth-chart of his client and conveys to him the results, what he does - or can do - is to change to some extent the *orientation* of the client toward the basic foundations and possibilities of his life. Such a change of orientation can have far-reaching effects. In some cases it might be as effective as if the person were suddenly brought in contact with a new religious or social outlook, which, if eagerly accepted, would transform the substance or quality of his relationship to other men and to God. As the individual learns to see the constituent parts of his own personality in a new light, as he comes to reinterpret his obvious and painful weaknesses, his disturbing conflicts and his unclear hopes, by considering them in relation to each other, his attitude toward the failures, assets, gifts and aspirations which he counts as his own is bound to be modified. This change of attitude or orientation will be a step either toward more effective integration or toward greater disintegration.

In other words, what the astrologer tells to his client will build in him a complex picture. This picture will act upon his consciousness in a way basically similar to that in which the vision of the crucified Savior dying to redeem man's sins acts upon the "pagan" ready to be converted to Christianity. It is a powerful symbol, and it acts as such. In acts upon the person's imagination, far more than upon his rational analytical faculties. It establishes a new allegiance, a new polarization of the will - which is always the servant of the imagination - perhaps a new faith ... or else, a new fear and a new sense of hopelessness or of optimistic self- indulgence.

The astrologer discussing the client's birth-chart is thus responsible for helping him to establish a new relationship between his

The *ninth step*

conscious ego and the potentialities inherent *in his total nature*. It is, or at least it can be, an enormous responsibility, and - as we saw previously - it is a responsibility which essentially does not stop with a brief astrological reading. However, this phase of astrological interpretation - the outlining of a picture of inherent individual potentialities as seen in the birth-chart and in no other way - presents a type of normal and spiritual responsibility quite different from that incurred when the astrologer makes definite forecasts for his client on the basis of a study of progressions and transits.

In the first case, the natal chart picture, if wisely presented, has to stand against what the client knows about himself. The client - if he is mature - can refute it on the basis of his own experience. If some points brought forth in the interpretation arouse in him a sudden feeling of recognition - if they "click" - this indicates that he was prepared to receive the knowledge or the revelation. Otherwise he will normally refute the astrologer's findings as nonsense and as a proof of the lack competency of the interpreter. He *can* refuse to believe the truth or adequacy of the picture of himself presented to him; in fact the average person confronted with such a picture often closes his mind to it, forgets it promptly, or twists it to suit his own ideas about himself. Thus, the danger of the picture having disintegrating and negative effect is relatively small, *provided* the astrologer does not lack utterly in the most rudimentary knowledge of psychology and of human nature; also, provided the client is not a hopeless neurotic ready to believe in anything simply because it is astrological, especially whenever it happens to strike the negative aspect of his personality.

The situation is different where prognostications are made to an individual, because in this case the individual has no recourse against the impact of such revelations. He is almost totally unprotected against their possible negative effect. Even if he reasons himself out of being consciously affected by the forecasts, his *subconscious memory* does not let go. This is worse obviously if the event or trend prophesied is unfortunate and if fear of its results is aroused - which is the case in nine cases out of ten! - but it can even have psychologically disintegrating effects when the thing expected is very fortunate, for it may lead to a self-satisfied expectancy blurring the edges of the individual's efforts.

As the astrologer seeks to "see ahead" in the client's life (and obviously this applies as well to his own life) he no longer deals with set and unchangeable celestial birth-patterns. He moves in a realm of forces in motion, of forever fluid relationship - a realm in which, in the first place, anything may happen because there is no way whatsoever of limiting the range of possible influences; and, in the second place, the kind of *expectation* which an individual has of the future is a powerful factor in determining what is actually to come. One should never forget this point.

No man lives alone. He is part of a family, a group, a nation - of humanity at large and ultimately of the entire universe. He acts upon that of which he is a part, but he is far more effectively acted upon by these various wholes of which he is a part. How, then, could an astrologer attempt to picture coherently and validly all these inter-related influences and mental impacts which assail any individual, especially in our wide open and chaotic twentieth century society? On the other hand, the future is not something that happens of itself outside of the individual. The individual's attitude towards it helps to create it; and this only makes it impossible to determine absolutely future events, it means that the astrologer assumes a great responsibility in conditioning his client's attitude toward the future.

All of which does not mean however that forecasts as such are unreliable and deceptive. Not only can it be proven statistically that predictions made by efficient and wise, thorough and personally unbiased astrologers hit a very fair percentage of accuracy, but one can easily see *how* astrological predictions can be correct and *in which way and within which kinds of limits* one can expect them to be reliable. The basic fact to keep in mind is that whatever happens to an organism (a body or a whole personality) can occur only within the limits of its capacity of response. Nothing can come out of a person which was not potentially within that person.

Translated into the language of astrological technique, this means that whatever may be the impact of planetary configurations and influences after birth, this impact will follow the lines of functional response shown in the birth-chart. Likewise whatever be the illness or unusual sense of exaltation which a man may ever experience, he will experience it with his body and psyche - thus, within the limits set by the basic "anatomy" of his physical and psychical organism. The fundamental structure of an individual personality is the "law" and the "truth" of that personality, and all that comes to the individual is conditioned by this law and this truth.

I said conditioned; I did not say fated. The events of the inner or outer life may be a *compensation* for inherent defects or weaknesses. A small opening or a solution of continuity in the fabric of personality may become, under the pressure of social or cosmic events, a gaping hole through which forces of evil pour. Nevertheless there must have been a weak point in the armor of the personality if this occurred. The weak point must register in the birth-chart, and if this intrusion of elemental or destructive forces occurs, the astrologer should be able to see (by means of his various methods of probing into the dynamic processes of human living) how and under what basic circumstances this intrusion took place. To know this, of itself, might be of no great value to the afflicted person; but the wise astrologer can discover, besides, the particular frame of reference within which it happened - thus essentially, *why* it happened.

Let us say that a Jewish citizen of Germany is persecuted and tortured during the Nazi regime. His individual reactions to the gruesome experiences are conditioned by what he inherently is as a human individual - thus, by the potentialities found in his birth-chart. He may survive the ordeal more or less intact in his personality, or he may lose his mind or die. The type of ordeal, the conditions in which it occurred, and the timing should be indicated by some astrological factor or group of factors. But the student of astrology must realize that *any number of factors* could refer to this type of tragic event. Powerful transits, a concentration of progressed aspects, eclipses, etc. might be the astrological indicators. No one could say *a priori* and ahead of time which would be the fatal symbols and still less whether the Nazis would be at the time ruling Germany!

What is even more significant, psychologically and spiritually, is that the persecuted Jew might have suffered primarily, either because he was an individual predisposed to certain types of personal tragedies, or because he was a Jew living in Germany. For the individual to know that, indeed, is of great *spiritual* importance; for he can thus determine the "frame of reference" of his tragedy and the scope of his response to humanity and the universe - and, as a result the scope of his responsibility (viz. his capacity for response).

The modern psychologist who belongs to Carl Jung's school of thought will at once realize the significance of the above statements, for he is accustomed to differentiate between the "personal" and the "collective" unconscious, and to refer the indications derived from dreams and other psychological factors to either field. The astrologer must evolve some similar type of technique if his interpretations and prognostications are to be of real value to his client. Above all, he should understand that the value of astrology - psychologically speaking, at least - does not reside in his ability to tell what is *likely* to happen (he can never say more!) as much as to help the client to understand fully and in terms of his total being what is happening, or has already happened.

Practically no one ever knows what his "total being" is. Most people live in a few corners of their nature, respond only with the periphery of their being, and never use more than a very small fraction of their brain cells and, in general, of their inherent potentialities. A birth-chart is such an abstract symbol (dealing only with a few basic functions) that it is impossible for the astrologer actually to deduce from it all that a client should like to know about his potentialities. Here is where the use of the progressions and transits comes in; for by studying them the astrologer may be able to learn *which* of these many potentialities will be accentuated through the process of actual living, which ones will focus the attention of the native or be brought to his attention by the pressure of his personal and social relationships. He may learn also approximately *when* these focusings will take place, and under what general type of circumstances. This knowledge, if properly used, can contribute to the attainment of a fuller, richer more total personality.

What happens to us is what needs to happen to us. As we go on living and experiencing, we relate ourselves with men, with collectivities and with a universe which is dynamic and impersonal. We encounter historical tides, waves and undertows. They move according to vast social and cosmic rhythms. Like radios being tuned in on this wave-length or that other, we experience these historical waves according to our own ability to respond to them - our selectivity. The "progressed aspects" made by our planets indicate changes in tuning and in our modes of response. But we can get through our receiving apparatuses *only what is there*. We may tune in to a wave of Uranian rebellion against binding relationships. The astrologer can tell us when we shall do it; but he cannot tell us what this Uranian wave will bring to our conciousness. It may be a local political fight, or an opening for a new demonstration of our capacity for initiative. It may be a planet-wide upheaval.

The former instance might stir us into the type of responsive action which would give us local prestige and power - the local frame of reference being something which we can constructively encompass and successfully deal with. But we might be a German Jew living during the years of national or world-wide persecution; and in this case, our rebellious Uranian response to life would probably lead us into situations, and against collective forces, which we are utterly unable to meet constructively. We are overcome; the Uranian crisis has proved destructive but no one could have predicted the substance and social circumstances of such a tragedy. What could have been predicted is only that we would tune in at such a time to a Uranian type of historical wave. Most of us can handle a small town's historical processes; very few can deal with world history and retain their integrity or health.

As we shall see presently, progressions deal theoretically with the way we tune in to the various wave-lengths of experience and create our opportunities, while transits refer primarily to the impact of the outside world upon us - that is, to the realizations forced upon us by our participation in the various private and public groups to which we have voluntarily given (or been compelled to give) our allegiance. Yet, in practice the two types of astrological factors are constantly interwoven. We cannot separate their effects, no more than we can separate the fact that we act as whole persons, according to an individual rhythm of growth or disintegration, from the fact that we act as parts of human groups and collectivities which move us and mould us, whether we are aware of it or not.

We should also never lose sight of the fact that we obey a definite rhythm of organic development, within a basic span of life, simply because we belong to the human species, genus *homo sapiens*. Thus planetary progressions and transits should be interpreted with reference to the human possibilities defined by the *age* of the individual.

In view of all this, we must therefore conclude that while the determination of the abstract nature of our individuality (the spatial pattern of our birth-chart) is a theoretically simple matter (even though becoming very complex if one attempts to bring the abstract indications to the level of basic *actualities* of temperament and character), the determination of the manner in which this individuality becomes revealed and fulfilled throughout the intricate cycles of life is most difficult. It is actually an impossibility, if by "determination" we mean the description of series of exact events to be expected as fated occurrences.

A single human individual represents a small cycle within an unending series of larger cycles, concentric and eccentric. All these cycles interact and interpenetrate. Nothing is isolated. No organism grows in a vacuum from birth to death, from seed to seed. All that the astrologer can reveal, while studying the case of an individual, is the time when the rhythm of this individual's cycle will become modified by inherent organic changes or by the results of having become related and open to the energies streaming from larger organic wholes of which he has become a part, consciously or unconsciously, willingly or unwillingly.

No one can tell in advance what these results will be. Once the door is open, once the relationship is made (or broken), *almost anything* may happen. It happens - it is true - essentially in one particular direction, or in its polar opposite; but the exact nature, and especially the scope, extent and implications of the happening are incalculable. They canot be known simply because one cannot know how the next larger organism will itself be related, at the time, to still larger ones. You open the dike through which the water of the stream connects to a river, which connects with the sea. You expect a few cubic feet of water; you may have to face a tidal wave. You expect a trout - and behold here is a man-eating shark! Astrology, as we know it today, cannot determine which of the two eventualities will come. It can only inform you that you will want to open the dike at a certain time - and most likely will open it. From then on, the risk is yours.

In another sense, the prediction is of the same nature as that which the astronomer makes of the coming of spring at the time of the equinox. Spring will come: this is a general, abstract statement. But the actual concrete results of spring - warmth, green leaves, flowers, and a happy sense of rebirth - may come late in February or in April, because the precise crossing of the equator by the sun, while basic, is not the only factor in the change of climate and the growth of planets. Spring will come; but what kind of spring? What will it bring to mankind? To this also the astronomer can give no answer.

Likewise the astrologer can see that a definite number of days or years after the individual is born, Jupiter and Saturn will interact in the form of a square. From this and other factors he can deduce that a crisis in the development of the individual will come during a certain year - or a little before, or a little later after. He may estimate with fair accuracy the basic character of the crisis, of the human need which it will focus, of the general type of individual activities and of circumstances which will be involved in that crisis. What he cannot foretell is, either what exact events will bring the crisis to a focus, or the manner in which the individual will respond to its challenge.

Every crisis is a challenge. Every definite progressed aspect or transit is an opportunity for transformation, expansion or purification. It is a door which opens upon the vast ocean of life and of the collective, universal unconscious. The main task of astrology is to help us to meet what comes to us through the threshold, and not that of speculating on some still remote openings of doors as yet unrecognizable. Every step forward - every crisis of growth - is a loss of balance at once counteracted by an equilibrium-restoring effort. If one tries to take two steps at a time, *one falls*.

The wise man knows this. He has no concern for problems which have not yet come. Yet in his understanding of the cyclic activity of nature he can take an impersonal long range view of things. By studying nature and nature's cycles he prepares himself to meet whatever nature has in store for him or for any other person to whom he is related. He learns the laws of change, he refuses to cling to forms and to fear the challenge of the new. He also refuses to worry about the new which is not yet born, not perhaps even conceived. He is wise, because he is as free of the future as he is of the past.

Such a wisdom is as difficult as it is rare. Yet without it, predictive astrology serves no valid psychological purpose.

The Study of Transits and Natural Cycles

Transits vs. Birth-chart

For many millennia the one great spiritual effort of mankind has been to realize the full and actual significance of two basic ideas. The first was that the world of change should not be considered (and feared) as a chaos of energies senselessly forming and dissipating themselves, but instead as an ordered realm of universal activity in which motion is inherently periodical or cyclic - even when it does not appear to be so to our superficial senses and, even more, to our disturbed and fear-ful emotions. The second basic concept is that, if one knew how to define cycles properly, one would see that *each cycle could be considered as the life-span of one specific type of entity retaining specific characteristics, biological or psycho-spiritual, during the entire cycle.*

It was on the basis of this second concept that the millennial efforts of the spiritual leaders of mankind have progressed, to the end that every man be able to realize himself as a *permanent identity* - permanent, that is, through the entire span of a cycle. We see the concept developing in ancient Asia and Chaldea, first, by building up the image of cyclic gods (AEons), gods who operate from the beginning to the end of immense cosmic Ages - time having become divided into periods of divine manifestations and periods in which the gods sleep, reawakening when the new cosmic dawn occurs.

However, after millennia of mental development, a few men began to think of a Supreme Being *who did not sleep* during the periods of universal dissolution or rest; who not only maintained the integrity of his self throughout all conceivable phases of time, but also remained active in a mysterious and transcendent way. About five thousand years ago, Hindu philosophers and Yogis came to the further realization that such a mysterious and transcendent condition of being need not remain unknown. They taught that man is inherently identical in essence with the Supreme Being, and therefore that he need not be the slave of sleep or death. Man could remain his self beyond the close of the life-cycle in which he emerged as an individual. He could bestride cycles and *know his self God* - if he were willing and able to submit to very rigorous disciplines of behavior and thought.

In this evolution of the spiritual consciousness of man, astrology played a most momentous part. It gave, first of all, the visible and demonstrable proof that the first of the two great concepts above-mentioned was correct - i.e. the proof that time was cyclic, that change meant a periodical sequence of measurable and predictable transformations or metamorphoses. Astrology, later, provided also an at least symbolical representation of the concept that every man is a potential individual; that is, that there is, in him, beyond all superficial change of moods, temperament and character, a *permanent structure of individual being*. This permanent structure *must* be there, if there is to be "individual immortality". It is the unchanging identity - the "archetype" - of the individual person at the core of all bio-psychological changes. It is the astrological birth-chart.

The birth-chart does not change, but the world goes on and celestial bodies pursue their cyclic motions as if nothing had happened. Yet something tremendous has happened; a man has been born with the *potential* ability to stop time in himself and to immortalize the structure of his selfhood - the structure patterned after the entire sky at the moment of his firs breath. If he succeeds in so doing, he becomes, actually and as a living human personality, his own sky - that is, God's projection upon the earth of one phase of His universal being at one moment of time. Individual immortality is thus the overcoming of the constant fatality of change by something which resists change - or, abstractly speaking, the overcoming of time by space. This means also the overcoming of "Nature" by "self", for self is the unchanging identity of the individual - the "I"; and the "I" is fundamentally the stable structure of being to which every changing factor has to be referred if there is to be *consciousness*.

If the "I" and his celestial representation (or "signature"), the birth-chart, do not change, Nature, on the other hand, is perpetual change. It is the multitudinous expression of the interplay of forces and energies forever waxing and waning, configurating themselves into what we perceive as bodies (from molecules to planets), then disassociating themselves and letting the evanescent material entities crumble away. Thanks to astrology (and to the sciences which grew from it) we know now that Nature is ordered; its manifestations are cyclic and measurable by the regular motions of celestial bodies. Knowing this, we need not fear these natural changes - old age and bodily death among them - and yet, we have to realize that to maintain (and perhaps to immortalize) our individual selfhood means *to overcome Nature,* its ceaseless transformations and disintegrations and its universal tendency to run down to a dead level ("entropy").

Astrologically speaking, this means that the integrity of our birth-chart should be maintained against the pressure of the universe of change (Nature) - thus, against the further dynamic impact of all celestial bodies altering their positions after our birth. These constant impacts refer to what astrologers call "transits". *A transit is the focused manifestation of the unending pressure applied by Nature upon the natal, archetypal structure of our selfhood.* It pits the power of the universe of change - and of the collective, social factors in individual experience which constitute "human nature" - against the integrity of the individual; thus it pits the ephemeris against the birth-chart!

All transits (except the passages of planets over the places they occupied in the birth-chart) tend to distort and disfigure the basic pattern of our self, to throw it out of balance. They are therefore challenges. If we meet them and remain true to our own archetypal "truth" (which can be read in the birth-chart), then we have gained greatly in consciousness and in power. We have learnt, by overcoming change or opposition, more about what we are as a changeless self. We are thus able to live a fuller life, to incarnate more of our self into earth-life, to express more convincingly our character, *to become in act what we are in potentiality* - which is the foundation for "personal immortality".

The Techniques of Transits, old and New

These statements can be made clearer and more workable when we consider the technique by the means of which the astrologer studies these transits. Having before him the birth-chart calculated for the exact moment of the first breath (the first moment of independent existence as an individual) the astrologer opens his ephemeris. If he wishes to determine the transits in force at any particular time in relation to this chart, he looks at the ephemeris for that year and day and he notes the zodiacal positions of all the planets. He then places them within the unchanging "frame of reference" of the birth-chart, and sees in wich houses they fall. He also calculates the angular relationships formed between these new planetary positions and the positions the planets occupy in the birth-chart.

Let us imagine that, in the birth-chart being considered, Neptune was placed on Cancer 19°48' (August 1, 1910). On May 5, 1946, according to the ephemeris, Saturn is to be found at the same zodiacal point, Cancer 19°48'; Jupiter is located ninety degrees away on Libra 19°48', opposed by Mercury passing then through Aries 20°. The astrologer will then say that Saturn is transiting over the natal Neptune; that both Jupiter and Mercury are forming by transit squares to this natal Neptune. Also about

106

the same time Mars will make a conjunction by transit with the natal Sun (on Leo 7°).

The astrologer will consider these several transits and seek to determine the meaning of each; then, he will try to coordinate the indications thus obtained into a more or less coherent picture of what the native may expect on or close to that day, May 5, 1946. He will say that the power of the transiting Saturn, superimposing itself upon that of the natal Neptune, will affect whatever Neptune stands for in the natal chart - perhaps his social consciousness, or his awareness of spiritual values, or his subconscious. If there is a predisposition to illness related to the natal Neptune-in-Cancer position, Saturn is likely to harden or consolidate such a tendency; but also if Neptune-in-Cancer signifies a diffuse and unsteady awareness of home responsibilities, Saturn, by moving over this natal Neptune, may compel the native to assume a more steady attitude, even though it may be under painful and somewhat oppressive conditions.

The transit of Mars over the natal Sun in Leo would be interpreted, on the other hand, as an emotionally stimulating and fiery indication; while the fact that Jupiter and Mercury square by transit the natal Neptune would tend to increase the social and mental pressures upon the native. In other words, the relationships between each "transiting planet" and each "natal planet" will be considered and interpreted according to the traditional meanings listed in text-books, old and new.

Besides this strictly analytical method there are, however, other approaches to the study of transits. The one that has been most validly demonstrated of late is based on a consideration of the cyclic relationship by transit of the moving planets to all the natal planets, and also on a study of the meaning of the periods of life defined by the stay of the transiting planets in each of the twelve houses, or each of the four quadrants of the birth-chart.

In the example above-mentioned, Saturn at birth was located at Taurus 6°18'. Because the sidereal period of Saturn averages 29 years and 9 months, this planet, moving in the zodiac after the day of birth, will return to its natal place in about 30 years. As its motion is watched within the frame of reference of the birth-chart - that is, as the astrologer scans through the pages of the ephemeris, month after month and year after year - it will be seen that this moving Saturn will come in conjunction with every planet of the natal chart and will cross successively every house. Thus, if an entire 30-year cycle of the moving Saturn around the fixed birth-chart is plotted, "critical periods" will be discovered; that is, the years and months when this Saturn makes strong aspects to the natal planets, and when it passes from house to house - and especially from quadrant to quadrant (the 4 "angles" of the chart, defining these quadrants).

In other words, whatever Saturn represents in the chart - the Saturn-function in its individualized expression - can be seen *evolving* through a 30-year period of the individual's life, as a result of the manner in which it finds itself related to the other planetary functions within the personality. Every planet has its own cycle, and the same procedure can be followed with each. Thus while the birth-chart indicates the *starting point* of these functional activities (the heredity factor, primarily), the transits indicate their *continual evolution* from birth to death.

Such an interpretation of the meaning of transits is entirely sound and valid. Yet it fails to realize that the birth-chart is *the unchanging archetype of the individual selfhood,* and not only the original and fundamental *starting point of a person's life.* The birth-chart, being such an archetype, establishes a goal. However, this goal is constantly clouded by the interplay and by-play of the unconscious and elemental energies of nature - unless the individual succeeds in clarifying and strengthening his realization and understanding of this divine goal meeting successfully the challenge of nature and of change.

What the actual events of a human life are and will be depends upon the everyday outcome of this contest or conflict between self and Nature, between the individuality structuring from within the human person and the pressure of everchanging collective and cosmic forces, of society and climate - *between the birth-chart as a whole and the entire sky, as pictured in the ephemeris during the years following birth.*

To study planetary transits is to compare the birth-chart and the "state of the heavens" at any selected time; and on this all astrologers basically agree. Where they differ somewhat is on the manner in which they interpret the relationship between the two factors being compared. In my estimation the transiting motions of the planets after birth do not represent directly an *evolution* of the functions, the individual character of which was indicated by the natal positions and aspects of these planets, but rather a *challenge* to the structure of the birth-chart considered as an unchanging archetype of individual selfhood.

Let us consider a birth-chart in which Jupiter is in sextile to Saturn. From my point of view, the motion of Jupiter after birth, revealed by the ephemeris, will tend to blur and distort the natal Jupiter-Saturn relationship (thus, the archetypal form and goal of the social or religious functions in the individual, his orientation to communal interchanges, his sense of social-personal stability and security - all things being connected with this Jupiter-Saturn relationship). The birth-chart defined the character and purpose of the relationship as a "sextile". Yet life, day after day, tends to alter this definition, by transforming the relationship - making it a square, an opposition, etc. Does this mean an "evolution" of the relationship? I say that it means instead a "challenge" to the individual as a whole, of whose permanent spiritual character the Jupiter-Saturn sextile was an integral part.

The change in the positions of Jupiter or Saturn will mean, however, a *strengthening* of the natal individuality when the planets return to their natal positions, and also, when the aspect between Jupiter and Saturn in the sky is once more a sextile - two entirely distinct occurrences. A challenge, however, may mean - as we already saw - either an increase in consciousness, if successfully met, or a blurring of the basic spiritual pattern of individual selfhood and character. Which of the two alternatives will be the fact is something almost impossible to determine with any degree of accuracy; this impossibility, indeed, is the mark of the individual's spiritual freedom. What *can* be fairly well determined, nevertheless, is the nature of the challenge and the general type of circumstances in which it will take place.

When in August 1921, Franklin D. Roosevelt was struck with infantile paralysis the fateful power of natural energies, of climate and viruses presented him with an awesome challenge. If we look for astrological transits to interpret the meaning of such a challenge, what do we find? A conjunction of Mars and Neptune in Leo and in the eleventh House in opposition to Roosevelt's natal Sun and Part of Fortune, and in square to his Saturn-Neptune-Jupiter grouping in the eighth house - a conjunction of Sun and Mercury on Leo 29°49' at the entrance of the twelfth house, in opposition to his natal Mercury (the chart's ruler) and in square to his Mars in the tenth house - a conjunction of Jupiter and Saturn on his Ascendant (according to the birth-time given in his father's diary).

Following the first method of estimating these transits the astrologer would take them one by one and evaluate their strength and meaning. For instance, the Neptune opposition to the natal Sun impairs vitality, and Leo and Aquarius suggest spinal and heart trouble as well as injury to the legs. Moreover from the fact that Mars is conjunct Neptune we may infer a sudden and pernicious type of occurrence, which - as Saturn, Neptune and Jupiter are squared - is likely to affect adversely social position and strength, etc.

The conjunction of Jupiter and Saturn on the natal Ascendant is a transit from which many things can be deduced, if considered alone. It could mean a new responsibility, a linking of personal destiny to national destiny; it implies indeed, a challenge. But what kind of a challenge, and how can we expect the individual to respond to it? The newer methods of transit-analysis will help us to answer these questions.

We can consider the transiting cycle of Saturn as a whole and we can say that the coming of Saturn to the Ascendant releases some kind of a seed of futurity which, however, will not germinate and grow until Saturn reaches the Nadir of the natal chart and begins to climb up the chart toward the Descendant and the zenith. Thus the Saturn transit is shown as one critical phase of the 30-year Saturn cycle - and similarly the Jupiter transit over the Ascendant, as a critical phase of a 12-year cycle.

We can go a step further. Jupiter and Saturn were conjunct in Roosevelt's natal chart. Such a conjunction recurs every 20 years (or approximately so, considering the retrograde movements of the planets). If we refer to what I stated before, the conjunction of 1921 should be understood as having *strengthened* Roosevelt's individual selfhood because, here, "Nature" (in its summer 1921 condition of change) repeated the pattern which is found in the structure of his permanent "self" (the birth-chart). Likewise the Jupiter-Saturn conjunction of 1940-41 restated Roosevelt's social prestige and he was re-elected for an unprecedented third term or office. The strengthening in 1921 was further defined by the fact that it occurred in relation to the Ascendant; the conjunction then drew forth the strength of the original will of the individualized spirit that was F. D. Roosevelt. But, in 1940-41, the strengthening was social and based on the fruits of his associations with fellow-workers, because the conjunction occurred in the eighth house (that of fruition of relationship) and in conjunction to Neptune. The strengthening was also particularly great in that the new Jupiter-Saturn conjunction occurred in the same area as the natal one.

This type of analysis may be applied to the above-mentioned Mars-Neptune conjunction which occurred as F. D. Roosevelt was stricken with paralysis. In his birth-chart Mars retrograde in the tenth house was in *semi-square* aspect to Neptune in the eighth; but in August 1921 Mars and Neptune came to a conjunction on Leo 15° in the natal eleventh house (social aspirations, hopes and wishes, etc.). Thus, because the semisquare is a sign of arousal and mobilization. Roosevelt's task, according to his archetypal pat-

tern of selfhood and purpose, was to mobilize his professional initiative and mental power of penetration (Mars in Gemini and the
Tenth House) in an effort to arouse his people (the Neptunian
collectivity) to the need for regeneration (eighth house Neptune)
and for a "new deal" in social organization (Jupiter-Neptune-Sa-
turn conjunction).

When August 1921 came "Nature" tried to pull the natal Mars-
Neptune semi-square toward the condition of a conjunction - thus
to alter and distort Roosevelt's individuality and spiritual purpose
by sapping (Neptune) the very foundation of his hopes to achieve
his ideal of Martial leadership (Mars-Neptune in the eleventh
House). This was the challenge of Nature to his self. Because
Roosevelt met it successfully and individualized in himself the need
for a new society (the Jupiter-Saturn force being "assimilated" by
his natal Ascendant), the challenge of the August 1921 sky to his
individual self led to a far greater consciousness of spiritual power
and purpose.

Much more should be said to show the possible practical application of the concepts I have attempted briefly to define; but I trust
that the general principle has been made clear. What the transits
and the geocentric pattern of the solar system day after day reveal
is the constant pressure exerted by all the collective and unconscious
factors which perpetually challenge the stability of an individual's
character, purpose and essential selfhood. Yet, there is magic in
such a pressure of Nature against the boundaries of the individual
self, similar to the pressure of the sea against the organisms which
live therein. By resisting this pressure man can become fully conscious of his self and his God-appointed purpose. By being confronted with the impact of a Nature which moves on, impassible and
mysterious, clothed in the unending sweep of cycles of birthing and
dying, man is under the compulsion to make himself immortal - or
to disintegrate together with all seasonal growths.

Nature, change, time are so many names for this compulsion -
which Hindus called *"maya"*, illusion. But *Maya* is also Mary, universal motherhood, the sea - by overcoming which, the "likeness of

God" latent in every man can become individualized and incorporated into an immortal personality. The astrology of transits plots for us the path to our immortality on the pages of the ephemeris, because it outlines for us that which we shall have to overcome and to assimilate. If it does detail with certainty concrete events, it is because what we call "events" are the results of the meeting of our individual selfhood and purpose with the many waves, eddies and undertows of Nature. Nature alone will not produce events. It is our contact with it - whether it be conflict or mating - which gives rise to events. Fate is only one of two partners in life: the divine Idea, that is our individual core, is the other. Every event registers our God's victory, or his defeat - until the contest is tried again.

Transits of Uranus, Neptune, Pluto

Some of the challenges represented by transits have a long-range objective. The changes they can bring about in our personality are slow in showing up. Their ultimate results are almost beyond us, beyond the possibility for us to experience them to the full in our short life-span. Yet we can see them unfolding - whether they tend to disintegrate our body, or to immortalize our personality - even if we cannot or dare not see the ends of these processes. I am speaking here of those challenging processes which can be measured by and are an expression of the sidereal cycles of the remote planets, Uranus, Neptune and Pluto.

Uranus revolves around the Sun in 84 years; Neptune in nearly twice the period (i.e. about 165 years on an average); Pluto in a little less than three times the same span (248.4 years). The relationship between these cycles (3-2-1) is quite extraordinary and must reveal some fact of profound significance. Mythological traditions speak of the "three steps" taken by the creative God at the beginning of the worlds; but this refers to the process of concentration of universals into particulars. In terms of the individual's evolution, the three trans-Saturnian (i.e. beyond Saturn) planets symbolize the three phases of a process of universalization which - if successful - frees the consciousness from the limitations and the narrow focalization imposed upon it by the Saturnian rigidity of the ego.

I have said that the continued year-by-year motion of the planets after birth represent ever-changing "Nature", in contradistinction to the "individual selfhood" defined by the birth-chart. But, according to all religious or occult teachings, man is that being within whom two kinds of nature come in contact and eventually should become integrated, the focus for the integration being the Saturnian ego. We may call these two natures celestial and earthly, or by any other name we choose; essentially they refer to the two poles of all consciousness, the universal and the particular. The cyclic motions of the trans-Saturnian planets symbolize the pressure of "universal Nature" upon our limited ego; those of the other planets (from Saturn to the Sun), the pressure of our particular type of organic, earth-conditioned, human nature. The Uranus-Neptune-Pluto transits challenge us to become *more than man;* the other transits, to become *bigger and better men.* The distinction is a very significant one.

The main cycle with regard to the former process (the becoming "more than man") is that of Uranus, because it alone may be spanned during a normal human life - exceptions notwithstanding. This cycle divides itself into 12-year and 7-year periods - the twelve 7-years periods referring mainly to the development of the higher facets of character, the seven 12-year periods dealing largely with changes in our social and financial outlook (as the 12-year cycle is essentially a Jupiterian cycle). These periods are related to the aspects which the moving Uranus makes to the position of Uranus in the birth-chart. Roughly speaking, Uranus comes by transit in opposition to its natal place when a man is about 42 - and this refers to the psychological crisis of the forties, the psychological (if not biological) "change of life" in men and women alike. Square-aspects by transit occur around 21 (the "coming of age")and around 63 (the "age of philosophy", the ingathering of all biological energies toward a spiritual "seed" - or their crystal-lization into a state of senility).

These crucial age-periods witness *challenges to metamorphosis,* challenges to become as an individual more than what collective man is at present - thus, to transcend the norm of present-day mankind (even of the cultured, intelligent average). These challenges operate, generally speaking, through the release of mental or psychic stimulants which tend to make us dissatisfied with what we are, and thus which challenge indeed our ability to reach beyond, or (as Nietzsche wrote) "to jump beyond our shadow". The jump may mean breaking our neck, but it does lead men to new realms of consciousness now and then!

These transit periods apply to all human beings, and thus are "generic". But the aspects which the moving Uranus makes to the other planets of the birth-chart refer to "individual" opportunities for growth - or to partial loss of personal integrity, if the pressure is not used constructively. Whenever the transiting Uranus meets a planet, the function represented by this planet tends to be highly stimulated or upset; the challenge of "higher Nature" is for this function to operate at a *more universal level.* All Uranian revolut-ions have this transcendent goal. If it is not reached, then the revolution results merely in an external change which changes nothing in reality, or in a meaningless upset.

The passage of Uranus by transit through the four quadrants of the birth-chart - and through each house - provides also basic in-dications, as it establishes a four-fold rhythm of spiritual unfold-ment and gives added meaning to the house-position of Uranus at birth.

What Uranus sets in operation, Neptune substantiates - which may mean either the dissolution of Uranus-shaken Saturnian walls, or the gestation of the transcendent universalistic seed projected by Uranus. Whenever Uranus comes by transit to Neptune such a Uranian fecundation can occur - which does not mean that it necessarily will, human inertia being what it is! In most cases Neptune does not even reach by transit the opposition-point to its natal place. In other words, the Neptunian challenge to the Saturnian ego *proceeds at most only half-way in a life-time;* the other half deals with the after-death conditions which the ego meets, and which challenge this ego to a type of growth (or dissolution) of which we know, alas! very little indeed.

Pluto's transit-cycle is only at most a third completed during even a long life. While Uranus acts characteristically as a one-pointed, straightforward drive, Neptune's action is two-dimensional - spreading like oil - and Pluto's power operates like a whirlpool, in spiral-like suction or explosion. Pluto's challenges, if they are to be met successfully, demand of man an unusual power of structural integration. Either explosive energies are to be contained within a strong "engine" and their use controlled, or the individual must stand in utmost firmness to resist being drawn into some kind of whirlpool. Whenever Pluto crosses by transit an angle of the natal chart, a strong demand is usually made upon the individual as to the nature of his essential life-purpose. Where Pluto is, there is the key to man's *greatest contribution to society,* and to the universe.

Transits of Saturn and Jupiter

These two planets define an individual's place and participation in society, or in any larger whole in which the individual operates as a functional part. Their transit-cycle establishes opportunities in social participation as well as changes in the place one occupies in society or in any permanent collective organization (for instance a religion, a traditional political Party, etc.).

Saturn establishes the individual's rightful and secure "place" in the collectivity and also his subjective sense of "I" resulting from such a placing in the greater whole. Saturn's cycle of nearly 29½ years can be repeated three times in a normal life-span, and these three cycles correspond approximately to the complete Uranus period. Here again we find the "three steps" pattern already mentioned. These three Saturn cycles *theoretically* represent the three successive polarizations of a man's ego at the three basic levels of selfhood - biological, psycho-mental and spiritual. At the first level, Saturn is the physical father; at the second (from 29½ to 59), the individual ego; at the third the divine Father-hood (59 to 88) - or rather, Saturn is the *type of security* (and of consciousness of "place") which corresponds to one's reliance upon (1) the physical father, (2) one's individual ego, (3) God-the-Father. These three types may obviously be felt at any time, but each of them is normally *emphasized* (to a lesser or greater degree) during the corresponding life-cycle.

The consciousness of one's place in the family, or in the collective organism of society, or in the spiritual universe, unfolds through the cycle of transiting Saturn. The transit-pattern can be studied in the way which I briefly described with reference to the Uranus transits. As Saturn moves from the one quadrant to another, changes occur in, both, one's subjective approach to the root-factors of individual being, and one's actual relationship to, or function in, society. When Saturn is in the first quadrant the best opportunities for inner repolarization generally occur. "Nature" or society, challenges man to reconsider his attitude to "self" - in the second quadrant to improve or renew his techniques of expression - in the third quadrant, to spread out or deepen his base of operation - in the fourth quadrant, to stamp his image and his purpose upon society (i.e. to assume public responsibility), or reap the harvest of the past and prepare for future growth.

Jupiter's transit-cycle covers a period of less than 12 years on an average. It deals with *man's sense of participation in society* - his confidence while participating (which attracts to him success and expansion), or his doubts and hesitancy which attract failure and frustration). The 12-year period has been used to measure the pattern of a man's financial and social ups and downs - each period beginning when Jupiter returns by transit to its natal position, and each of the twelve years being considered as a "mansion" of Jupiter with characteristics similar to those of the regular twelve houses. The ordinary way of analyzing and interpreting transits through the four quadrants of the birth-chart is, however, as significant in Jupiter's case as in that of all the other planets.

Jupiter and Saturn are polar opposites. They are the basic factors which control the growth of social groups and nations within the scope of their particular, organic existence, because they refer to the social interdependence of individuals within their traditional and normal ability to participate in a collective organism. Every 20 years, Jupiter and Saturn come in conjunction, and this 20-year cycle has been considered in the past as basic, wherever the destinies of nations and kings were concerned. It is still significant today in terms of the tidal movement of man's social consciousness and social fortunes; but, in a world dominated increasingly by universalistic values and international factors, more fundamental indications are found in the cycles of Uranus, Neptune and Pluto - and still larger ones. Nevertheless, the places in which the Jupiter-Saturn conjunctions fall in a natal chart (at 20-year intervals) establish *foci of social destiny* which are highly significant, especially in the lives of individuals who seek and assume public responsibility.

Smaller Transit-Cycles

The transit-cycles of Mars and Venus last about two years. They include a period of weeks during which these planets are retrograde. The house (or houses) through which the planet moves back and forth are given a particular transit-emphasis. The challenge brought by "Nature" to the individual focuses itself there. It is primarily a personal challenge and an opportunity for the individual to reorient his desire-nature and his faith (Mars), and his sense of creative expression and of value, of attraction and repulsion (Venus) - especially when the planet crosses three times its natal position.

Mercury, being never more than 28° away from the Sun, has a transit-cycle not very different from that of the Sun. During this approximate year-cycle, Mercury experiences usually three entire periods of retrogression, which thus establish three zones of emphasis in the natal pattern of individual selfhood. Whenever the

118

character of these emphases can be recognized and understood, the individual should learn a great deal about his mental needs; but these are primarily subjective needs, and no one except the individual himself is likely to know their exact significance. However, the meaning of the houses in which the retrograde periods fall offers a basic clue. When Mercury transits back and forth over a natal "angle", the opportunity to develop the function which this angle represents is great - but it is an opportunity *under psychological stress,* and perhaps *in spite of* difficult environmental or health conditions. These remarks apply as well to the retrograde transits of Mars and Venus, these transit-phases referring often to the need for regeneration or reconsideration of attitude. The periods are not usually favorable for truly new departures; but they offer real opportunities for setting right - under pressure and with the risk of making matters worse - what had been wrongly or inadequately started.

The Sun and the Moon make their transits around the birthchart respectively in a year and in a lunar month (27½ days). It is often possible to establish a connection between the passage of the Sun and the Moon through each of the four quadrants of the birth-chart and a definite four-fold rhythm of the solar and lunar forces in a person's nature. The time when the Sun each year crosses the natal angles is often a challenge to the psychological functions these angles symbolize - thus precipitating certain types of events. The birthday period every year - and the day when, every month, the Moon returns to her natal position - can usually be considered as times when the innate solar and lunar characteristics are given a new emphasis or revivified. Indeed the making of "solar return" and "lunar return" charts has been very much emphasized of late - quite a few astrologers claiming that such charts provide the most accurate means for predicting life-events at the personal level.

Such charts are cast for the exact times at which the Sun and the Moon return to their positions at birth; but unless the very precise birth-time is known there is very little use in attempting to make such charts, because events during the solar year (or the lunar month) ahead are said to occur when planets cross the four angles of the chart. Usually the solar or lunar return charts are calculated for the place of residence at the time, but I am not certain that this is always the best method; it seems that the locality of birth gives better results.

I personally have found it just as significant simply to place the transiting planets at the time of the solar return on the outside of the natal chart and then to evaluate their relationship to the natal houses and planets. Yet if the exact birth-time is known it is no doubt worth while to calculate the zodiacal positions of the four angles of the solar return chart, and to see in what natal houses they fall.

Other techniques - and so many are possible - have value if they have a logical basis and when consistently used by a competent astrologer believing in their validity. For instance, the cycle of eclipses can give very significant indications in many cases. This is the Saros cycle of the Chaldeans, which measures the return of eclipses to approximately the same place in the zodiac (thus in the natal houses) every 18 years and 11 days. Eclipses result from an exact alignment of Sun, Moon and Earth. During a *solar* eclipse the Earth receives the full force of the soli-lunar conjunction. It constitutes an over-stressful challenge to start something new and to discard the old. It can mean either revolution or evolution, depending upon the strength of the inner structure of personality - that is, upon the individual's ability not to be violently torn away from his center.

Lunar eclipses, on the other hand, are challenges to personal integration. The Earth is pulled in exactly opposite directions by the Sun and the Moon; this can mean disintegration - or, as the Moon resurges from her ghostly appearance while eclipsed, a new adjustment to life, a new quality of integration of self with environment.

THE ELEVENTH STEP

The Study of Progressions

I have stressed throughout this book the fact that astrology is essentially a study of life-cycles, that is, a study of the structural order which can be detected in the time-sequence of events in the lives of individuals and nations. The concepts of cycles, of cyclic recurrence of phenomena and of periodical phases in the growth of living organisms would not have taken form in the human mind unless often recurring sequences of phenomena had been noticed. To notice such sequence, however, is one thing: to be able so to measure them as to be able to determine the precise pattern of their recurrence is another thing. All such time-measurements involve the use of clocks - exactly as space-measurements require a measuring rod, a yardstick.

Until the last few years the basic clock in *all* types of time-measurement has been the sky. The hands of that clock were originally the Sun and the Moon. Later on, when greater precision was required, the passage of stars at the zenith served as the basic measure of time. In any case, time was measured by the cyclic motion of some celestial body, as space was measured in reference to the dimensions of our globe; a common basis for all human experience was taken as the standard of measurement. Astrology is valid because the cycles it takes *as measuring rods for the many and varied processes of life-development* are matters of common human experience. It is valid in the deepest sense because these cycles have thus become imprinted in the ancestral, collective unconscious of mankind. They are root-factors in the mind of man.

121

What are these cycles? The day, the year, the lunation month - and in far broader and more recent way, the cycle of precession of equinoxes, that is, the cycle of the changing relationship between the timing of the seasons and the place of the Sun among the stars.

The day-cycle is the most basic period as it refers to the alternation of light (or activity) and of darkness (or rest). It was determined by the rising and setting of the sun. The year-cycle deals with seasonal changes, and it was measured by the change in position of the setting (or rising) sun, south and north of a middle position which was called west (or east). Zodiacal calculations came at a later date; what served originally to measure the year-cycle was, almost without doubt, this south-north oscillation of the setting-points of the sun at the western horizon. As for the lunation month, it was a cycle defined by the phases of the moon; thus by the interval between two new moons (or at first probably, between two full moons - more easily observable facts of experience).

In the preceding chapter I have stressed the basic opposition there is between the birth-chart as a permanent factor and the constantly changing pattern of the solar system during the years of a person's life. I said that it should be interpreted as the opposition between the permanent individual selfhood of this person and ever changing Nature, between the basic personal identity and the many forces which seek ever to challenge its integrity. We should, however, not overlook the fact that a man's identity is only an archetype, an abstract plan, a *constant* to which that which perpetually changes should be referred if there is to be consciousness and integrated development of personality.

There is an old saying to the effect that "a temple is not built in one day". The building of the temple is a process; and while we might say that this process depends upon two main factors, the blue-prints and the sum-total of the activities of the builders (subject to various pressures, moods and conflicting opinions or desires for self-expression), yet a third factor must also be considered. Without the architect's blue-prints as a constant frame of reference the activities of the builders would have neither cohesion, plan, nor purpose; but without a *schedule of operations* and the overseeing activity of a manager or contractor, the building process would not work out smoothly or efficiently.

A man is not born with an already made personality. Personality develops and includes essentially three factors:

(1) An individual pattern (blue-prints) which establishes the basic arrangement and purpose of the particular human organism being born.

(2) The interplay between, on the one hand, this permanent structure of selfhood and, on the other, the energies of human nature, the pressure of social-cultural traditions and needs, the impact of climate and earth-conditions, etc.

(3) A managing intelligence which seeks to make the second factor serve constantly the purpose of the first; to turn the *challenges* of changing nature into *opportunities* for personal growth.

The part played by this managing intelligence is an integrative one. The contractor-manager is he who sees to it that the blue-prints become a concrete building - through the work of the builders, through the proper cooperation of social-political agencies, through an adequate flow of materials, through all the constant adjustments required during the building process (i.e. during the life-long development of personality). Adjustments require contracts, compacts, covenants, consultations, coordination, correlation; and all these things are in the domain of intelligence.

Intelligence is the capacity to make workable and efficient adjustment to the inner as well as the outer environment. Intelligence integrates human, social experience so that it may be of use and meaning to the self, the "I". It manages (with the assistance of the will) the activities of the person. The deeper intelligence makes its adjustments by means of constant references to the original blueprints and purpose of the developing personality - while the superficial, opportunistic intelligence works in the very midst of natural forces and social pressures, seeking temporary solutions, soothing hurt feelings, dealing in compromises and diplomatic give-and-take.

What the astrologer generally calls "progressions" deals essentially with the operation of these two types of intelligence. It can be said - provided one does not take the point too literally - that the *progressions* as a whole reveal the means whereby the *transits* and the *birth-chart* can be integrated; or, perhaps more accurately, the workings of those agencies in the individual which seek constantly to incorporate the results of experience (transits) into the framework of the self (birth-chart). These agencies "belong" fundamentally to the self; they serve - or rather, should serve - the purpose of which the self is a manifestation. They carry out - if all goes well - the will of the self at every step in the progressive development of the personality.

At the moment of the first breath, we might say, God impresses upon the human organism His purpose and plan for this particular organism; this is the birth-chart. But in order that the integrity of this pattern (selfhood) be not rapidly shattered by the impact of human experience (transits), God keeps on an active watch over the nascent child. He actually leaves with the child, as an integrator and comforter, the Holy Spirit (the Hebrew *Shekinah*) - which is the "spirit of understanding", or intelligence.

The position of the Sun, at the time of the first breath, is the "Son of God" - the center of a man's selfhood. The development of this "divine seed" has taken normally nine months. Three months more, and the entire zodiacal cycle of the Sun will be completed. This three-months-after-birth Sun is the "progressed Sun". It is the progressive manifestation or revelation of God's Holy Spirit in man. It is divine Intelligence operating within the individual person as an integrative power: as the power to assimilate (without being overwhelmed or deviated by their impacts) the experiences of life in nature and in society.

The "progressed Sun" is indeed a progressive revelation of intelligence; and the integration of the personality is a process the very core of which is this gradual development of intelligence. The progressed Sun is intelligence and integration at work in the life of the growing personality. The span of this life is theoretically measured by the cycle of Uranus (84 years) - or from another point of view by one degree of precessional motion of the equinoxes (70 to 72 years). The motion of the Sun after birth up to the time when it reaches the zodiacal point at which it was *at the time of conception* takes normally about three months, or 90 days. During these 90 days after birth God's creative power operates directly by projecting the *seeds of intelligence,* by releasing the powers of the Holy Spirit within the potential personality.

Each day after birth is a release of such potentialities of integrative intelligence. What is released each day, generally speaking, will serve to meet the problems of experience-assimilation each year. These powers or faculties of the Holy Spirit within man constitute *the continuing outflow of divine creativeness after birth*. This outflow ceases when the solar cycle which began at conception is completed. Then, man has everything he needs *WITHIN HIMSELF* - as potential, as divine seed. All he has to do is TO USE IT.

If one thoroughly grasps the meaning of these statements one should find no basic difficulty in relating to one another the three basic factors used in modern astrology - birth-chart, transits and progressions. Nor should one be puzzled by the seemingly arbitrary concept of "one day after birth in the ephemeris corresponding to one year of actual living" - or by the abstract idea of the equivalence of the basic cycles of motion studied by astrology. This abstract equivalence of day and year - that is, of the periods of axial rotation and orbital revolution of the earth - is a logical concept; yet it involves a number of practical difficulties and, above all, it fails to give a vital and spiritual meaning to the "progressions". No one can significantly understand or use this factor of progressions if he considers it as a measuring rod for concrete *events*. Whether there are events or not to fit "progressed aspects" is not what matters. Progressions, as applied to the unfoldment of the human person year after year, refer to the gradual demonstration and actualization of those powers of understanding and of intelligent adjustment to life which were the "trail" of God's essential creation of the individual self of man at the time of the first breath.

The architect establishes the blue-prints. Then he summons a contractor; he discusses with him an orderly schedule for the many successive building operations - then, the contractor is given the money (power-energy) necessary to proceed. The progressed Sun is the contractor, the guide, the overseer. His work is completed by that of the progressed Moon, who is the dispenser of the spiritual energy required to meet the challenges of life-experiences. The progressed Sun is intelligence in action; the progressed Moon, effective energy parcelled out to sustain the application of this active and integrative intelligence. *Neither of them represent directly events; but the potentiality of intelligent adjustments to events.* Obviously, without events there can be no adjustment to events. Thus the motions of the progressed Sun and Moon generally *correlate with events.* They do not *indicate* events as such, but only the release or actualization of the individual's ability to meet successfully the challenge of experience.

The Technique of Progressions

The calculation of progressions offers no great difficulty and is explained in many astrological text-books. If a person is born January 1, 1900 at noon Greenwich Time, the progressed Sun and Moon (and the progressed planets) for January 1, 1901 will have the zodiacal positions indicated in the ephemeris for noon, January, 1900. The motion of the progressed Sun during the first year of life covers thus about 1°1'; the progressed Moon, about 14°34' (from Capricorn 9°37' to 24°13'). During the second year of the person's life the progressed Sun and Moon will proceed to their ephemeris positions for January 3, 1900; during the third year, to those for January 4, etc. The progressed positions for any month of these years can be calculated by a simple proportioning of the zodiacal distance covered by the Sun, Moon and planets as they move from one noon ephemeris position to the next.

The progressed positions are usually recorded within an outer circle of the birth-chart. As the birth-chart remains the same, the progressed Sun, Moon and planets can be watched advancing year after year *through* the natal houses and the signs of the zodiac. This advance can be interpreted in two basic ways:

(1) As the progressed Sun, Moon and planets move from house to house, and sign to sign, new conditions arise and are interpreted according to the astrological nature of houses and signs. The symbols of the degrees can also be used as significant indications, particularly in the case of the progressed Sun.

(2) The progressed celestial bodies, as they move on, come to form aspects to the natal (or "radical") planets in the permanent birth-chart. They form aspects also between each other, aspects which differ from those the natal planets made to one another. Both types of progressed aspects can be considered significant and can be interpreted.

The study of progressions fails, however, to reveal the most vital conclusions that can be reached through this branch of astrology if a definite distinction is not made between the solar, the lunar and the planets' progressions; and moreover if all of them are not seen integrated within the cycle of the "progressed lunation".

Essentially, all progressions which are based on the symbolical equivalence of day and year are solar; simply because these two cycles are solar cycles. Progressions are symbols of the continuation of the revelation of light, which is birth. The impact of the "first breath" spreads through the entire organism, impresses itself, as it were, in concentric waves upon every cell. The birth-chart is the imprint; but the effect of the act of impression (or spiritual impregnation) takes time to manifest. Light (and air) penetrate slowly through all the layers of human nature. This "light" is solar and lunar. Solar light, in this sense, is intelligence in action; lunar light is energy released for organic purpose. The latter derives from the former which it *distributes*.

In the usual technique of progressions, the planets operate only as modifying agents. Only the planets close to the earth - Mercury, Venus and Mars - progress fast enough to be of real significance as progressed factors. Jupiter and Saturn can progress only a few degrees during a life-time, and unless their after-birth motions bring them to an exact aspect of great importance to a vital point of the birth-chart, their progressed positions can be ignored. Jupiter and Saturn refer essentially to social factors - to the individual's relationship to the larger whole of which he experiences himself a part. They act thus mainly through outside pressures - and as transiting factors. The aspects made by the progressed Jupiter or Saturn are subjective indications of a change of social or religious attitude which should be interpreted in connection with the transits of these same planets.

All progressions are essentially subjective, even though they correlate closely with objective events. The lunar progressions are those which refer the most closely, as a rule, to such objective life-happenings; but they denote *an activated potentiality of individual response along a certain line,* rather than actual events. The position of the progressed Moon month after month - in terms of natal house and zodiacal sign - indicates *the most vital focus of a person's attention* at the time. Obviously things will happen in the basement of the house being built, if the building-schedule calls for builders at work there. The schedule says nothing about possible accidents occurring there at the time; it reveals only a possibility of accidents in a particular location, *if* any mistake is made. The progressions refer to the schedule, not to the mistakes.

The most significant and consistent way of dealing with the progressions of the planets is to study them within the framework of what I have called "the progressed lunation cycle".* This is the cycle between two conjunctions of the progressed Sun and the progressed Moon (i.e. two progressed New Moons), and it encompasses nearly 30 years - approximately the same period as the cycle of Saturn's transits. This progressed lunation cycle is the cycle of

---

* Cf. my book "THE LUNATION CYCLE: A key to the Understanding of Personality.

personality-development, and it includes in their proper relationship the solar and lunar factors.

The progressed planets fit into the framework of this 30-year cycle. They modify the flow of solar intelligence and lunar energy-for-use. All personal adjustments to life are made on the basis of intelligence and of useable organic-psychic energy. Both are always "at hand"; but the "hands" may not grasp adequately what is before them - they may tighten up in fear or over-eagerness - they may hold, only to let go in confusion of what they held. The emotional factors which largely control these reactions are symbolized by the progressions of Mars and Venus, in so far as these modify the basic flow of solar-lunar potential.

The progressed Mercury refers mostly to the mental factors, to memory. If the progressed Moon indicates the focus of an individual's attention upon one field of experience or another, Mercury has much to do with the *focusing apparatus*. Particularly important are the years of life which correspond to a change in the direction of Mercury's motion (from direct to retrograde, or *vice versa*); but this change acquires its full meaning only if referred to the pattern of the whole progressed lunation cycle.

This pattern is determined by the house, sign and degree on which the progressed New Moon and Full Moon occur, and by the aspects which the progressed Sun and Moon make during the cycle with the natal planets - and secondarily, with the progressed planets. The aspects of the progressed Sun with the natal planets, and its passage from house to house and sign to sign, are the most basic factors - together with the crossing by the progressed Moon of the four angles of the birth-chart, especially the Ascendant.

Other methods of progressions have been devised; also what are called "primary directions" dealing with the motion of the horizon and meridian after the exact moment of birth. There is no doubt that anyone who is thoroughly familiar with any one of these systems and who focuses his attention constantly upon its type of results can achieve a degree of success in making forecasts and establishing "proofs" of its validity. This is because we live in a world defined by man's mind and man's perceptions, a world which answers our quest for order, because it is basically a projection of the order within our own human nature. Wherever we look we see only what we, as "humans", potentially are. Thus religions say that God made man in His image - another way of saying that there is a basic identity of character between the universe *as we experience it* (let us not forget!) and our generic nature.

For this reason, we live in a symbolic world. For this reason, it can be said truly that man creates his own destiny, and calls upon himself the events or experiences he needs for his development. We build our house; the plan and schedule of the building direct our steps. If we are wise, we move according to plan and schedule. We avoid strikes and accidents. The unwise always want to work on the fire-place, when it is time to dig the cess-pool! The astrology of progressions deals with the world which is ours, because it is the continuation of what we are. Its greatest validity is that it may help us to live *consistent lives,* in terms of solar intelligence, through the proper and timely use of the energy which is ours by birth-right.

THE TWELFTH STEP

The Significant Use of Horary Techniques

W hether we deal with transits or with progressions, we are considering the relationship of the individual as a whole to the general pattern of his experience and his personal development. We are dealing with generalities and potentialities, with categories of events and broad types of personal response. Neither transits nor progressions refer to exact particulars. Both planets and houses or signs can mean many and varied things, at several levels. The indications they give are never *of themselves* precise in terms of concrete events; they become precise only if the trend of the person's life and the issues to be met are already distinguishable and well established. The transits and progressions, then, reveal what can be expected in the line of such trends or confrontations. Otherwise, the astrologer can only surmise possibilities, the actualization of which might take place along any one of several lines. The focus of the astrologer's advice has to be upon the individual and his adjustments to life, not upon specific events or confrontations.

There is, however, a type of astrology in which particular confrontations, problems and crises, instead of being deduced as possibilities from general patterns of personal adjustment to life, are considered as primary factors and starting points. It is called "horary astrology" - the term "horary" meaning "of the hour".

Horary astrology is the astrology of particulars. It deals directly with stated particular cases and situations, and the individual person facing these particular setups of experience appears in horary

astrology in a special role. *He punches the clock* at the entrance
of the realm of conscious living; that is, he signifies his willingness
to start consciously to work on whatever problem is his at the
time. He establishes his need and his readiness to meet it in terms
of a universal purpose, to meet it with that intelligence which,
while it is *individualized* through an individual mind, is essentially
a universal factor.

The life of the average man and woman is conditioned by biological impulses or feelings, egocentric responses to experience, patterns of traditional behavior and socially expected reactions, and
by a confused or unsteady yearning toward some ideal state of
being. The individual may think about many things; he may even
have a brillant intellect quick at associating remembered data and
at reshuffling the cards filed for reference in his brain - and yet he
may not live in the least according to the "conscious way" of true
intelligence. He probably knows what he wants, and his intellect
may discuss the *pros* and *cons* of every life-situation in terms of
that "knows" and that "wants". He may display the kind of social
intelligence about which intelligence-tests give data - a ready faculty for adapting himself to social situations and the demands of collective living. But all this does not deal with what I call here
"conscious living". It refers only to biological, egocentric or social
behavior.

"Conscious living" means living as an individual, differentiated
from the average, conscious of a purpose, and determined constantly to adjust his life (behavior, feeling and thinking) to the
requirements of that purpose. If the individual sees himself as an
individual separated from all else in the world, and if his purpose
is egocentric and unrelated to anything greater than his self, we
have a kind of living which is negative, basically destructive, and
purposeful rather than conscious. *True consciousness implies a
deeply felt and acknowledged relationship between the individual
and the universe.* An individual unrelated to the universe is a
fiction. No individual lives in a vacuum. Related he is - to a group,
a society, mankind, the universe. If he is not fully aware of this

state of total relatedness he cannot be called truly "conscious", however brilliant his intellect, his social cunning and his success. He lives in terms neither of true intelligence, nor of spirit.

Intelligence is the focalization of universal harmony into the individual mind. It is the adjustment of the individual to the universal, of particular actions to the universal purpose which *alone makes them* spiritually significant. To live according to the "conscious way", the way of true intelligence, is to live in terms of one's essential place, function and purpose in the universal Whole. It is to will one's destiny; to become step by step the totality of what one potentially *is*. It is to fulfill the universal Harmony at the place and at the time one is called upon to act. It is to become, as a concrete personality on earth, one's natal Sky. It is to do so, not only in a general way, but every day, at every moment, with the greatest possible efficiency, accuracy and purity of motive.

But, how can we ever be sure that we are living in such a way? What standard of value, what frame of reference can there be against which we can test the validity of our acts *at the precise time* when we face a new test, a new crisis, a new problem? Astrology answers: "Consider the sky. Question its ordered patterns. Ask of the universal Harmony for an answer. Just as Nature has a cure for every ill, so the sky has a solution for every problem. Every individual need, consciously and clearly formulated, and stated with fervent eagerness, is always filled by the spirit - if the individual does not close his door to the spiritual influx and the divine message."

Intelligence, as I have defined it, is a universal factor. It is potential in every human being. It pervades the entire universe. All that is needed is for the individual to produce a "lens" able to focalize it, and a mind able to receive and contain its emanations. There are many kinds of lens and mental containers, but intelligence is one and the same everywhere. It is in every organic whole, as it is visible in the sky. If we can decipher it more easily in the sky, it is because, there, it is made simpler and more structurally clear by the remoteness of the celestial bodies, by the fact

133

that we - the questioners, the ones in need - cannot disturb the celestial patterns in any way; also, because the experience of the sky and of its lights is one of the most vital and most ancient among experiences common to all men.

However, what is essential is to know what we are seeking for; it is our attitude toward the seeking; and as well toward the answer we receive. What is essential is to realize that we can reach this intelligence *directly*, as it becomes focused into our mind, when we are ready for it, just as well as *indirectly* when expressed through our relationship to the universe and particularly to the solar system which is the "living space" of our Sun, source of our vitality. Intelligence is the active manifestation of universal Harmony; and therefore wherever disharmony is produced, there must also be an effort to re-establish harmony. This is the law of compensation, whether it be seen by occultists as *Karma*, or by psychologists as the principle of "psychological compensation" (C.G. Jung). Because of it, every emptiness must be filled, every need must be satisfied - provided there is not something in the empty vase or the person in need which blocks the way to the re-establishment of harmony.

It is on these principles that the true kind of horary astrology is based. Every horary chart cast *in answer to a need which is well-formulated and real* should be considered as an expression of universal intelligence seeking to re-establish the harmony disrupted by the crisis or the problem which caused the personal need. The person in need could have found a direct answer within himself if his mind had been effectively open to the influx of intelligence - call it "intuition" if you will, or "God's answer to his prayer". But if the individual's mind is too confused, cluttered or anguished to form itself into a "lens" to focus the universal intelligence constantly seeking to re-establish harmony, then an *intermediary* or a *mirror* must be found to do the focusing and the objectivizing. The intermediary (or "mediator") may be a spiritual Personage (a great Prophet, for the race at large, or a *Guru* - even a psychologist, if of the right kind - for the individual). It may be an astrologer able to decipher and interpret the "sky's signature" through the technique of horary astrology.

The technique is basically simple; yet exceedingly difficult to apply significantly, correctly and wisely. Horary astrology is an art. It needs to be practiced by individuals who have made of themselves - consciously, or sometimes unconsiously - channels for the expressions of universal intelligence; who have in one way or another - some ways are far safer than others! - reached a state of "openness to the world" and of inner tranquility, or of vibrant, yet detached, sympathy with human beings. The safe and sound practice of horary astrology requires a basic knowledge of its technique; but it demands also of the practitioner a deep sense of psychological values, and as deep a sense of responsibility to humanity as a whole and to God Who is the personification of this universal intelligence.

The practice of horary astrology rests upon the erection of a horary chart *for the exact moment at which a personal need comes to a focus of attention, or a personal crisis comes to a head.* The horary chart is cast like any birth-chart for the moment in consideration; but the interpretation of the horary chart obeys a number of rules which differ noticeably from those used in natal astrology. What these rules are has been stated most significantly and expertly by Marc E. Jones in his book "Problem Solving by Horary Astrology", and the interested reader is referred to it, as the matter is too vast to be considered here. I believe, however, that no horary interpretation can be complete and spiritually valid unless the interpreter realizes fully that horary astrology is not just a method - rather queer and mysterious - to get "one's problems solved" without much effort, but the expression of a profoundly spiritual attitude to life. Horary astrology is a practical technique based on a philosophy of reverent relationship to the universe and to that universal intelligence which most men consider as the very substance of the Deity. If the practitioner is not aware of that relationship and of the fact that every horary chart is a focalized expression of universal intelligence, then, even though the horary answer may be correct, the results are bound to be inadequate and sometimes tragic.

I said that as an individual asks the sky for an answer to a vital problem or crisis confronting him, he thereby, intentionally or not, signifies his readiness to meet the confrontation in terms of "conscious living". It should be clear, however, that this readiness exists in the average person who asks for horary advice only in a *negative* manner. The asking may be done because everything else has failed, or because there is no logical and intellectual way of ascertaining how events over which one has no control will develop, or because it is an easier way than to study deeply the matter, or in order to evade personal responsibility - or worse still, out of sheer curiosity. These are all negative attitudes.

The positive attitude might be characterized as an attitude of prayer. According to it, the individual seeks to ascertain the will of the universal intelligence with regard to the particular confrontation he is meeting. He does not seek to evade his responsibility, *but rather to increase his responsibility by making it as fully conscious as possible* by relating it to the universal purpose or "plan" of life, or of God. It does not lead to a blind and superstitious following of the answer revealed or suggested by the horary chart, but instead to a new adjustment of one's efforts in becoming conscious of the purpose behind the confrontation, and of all the factors implied in the issues.

A horary chart does not say: do this! It presents a symbolic image of all the essential factors in any critical situation, an image from which purpose to the patterning of these factors can be revealed - if the interpreter is able to see this purpose emerge. Sometimes the purpose - that is, the constructive directive or solution - is very evident. In most cases, it is not. It may require as great an effort of attention to decipher the answer outlined by a horary chart as would be the attempt to solve the life-problem by ordinary means. *Horary astrology is not a saving of effort, or intelligence; it is a reorientation of effort and intelligence.* It does not make life easier, but man more conscious of the total implications of the difficult turning points at which he has to make choices. It aims at providing a *universal dimension* to choices, instead of a strictly personal and narrow one - a "fourth dimension" of the will, in which time becomes a determinant and the proper timing of actions and decisions on the background of universal cycles is made possible, even in the smallest acts.

The act may be small, yet it must involve a *vital need* if the horary chart can be counted upon to give a vital answer. He who is to act must consider his questioning an implicit pledge to act consciously in an inner attitude of openness to the revelation of universal intelligence focused upon him, and to assume thereby a fuller responsibility for the actions. The responsibility is greater, in as much as the action ceases to be conditioned strictly by personal choice and becomes an expression of the guidance of this universal intelligence. He who does not know the total pattern cannot be blamed for not fitting into it. He who knows it breaks deliberately the structural harmony of universal life if he fails to live according to his knowledge.

So far, we have assumed that the person who is confronted by a vital problem or crisis is the one who erects the horary chart and seeks to discover in it the solution which the universe is potentially offering at any time to any seeker who asks in the right way. However, it is as difficult for the individual to interpret a horary chart erected to solve his own crisis, as it is for the average student of analytical psychology to interpret his own dreams. In either case we deal with the interpretation of symbols; and if the interpreter is subjectively involved in the crisis - if it is his own crisis - he is likely not to be *objective* enough to interpret the symbol without coloring the interpretation with his own emotional and intellectual biases or confusion.

Thus the need, in most cases, for an interpreter who should be a "mediator" between universal intelligence and the confused or impotent mind of the enquirer - a mediator who should be able to focus in complete mental tranquility and detachment the message of this universal intelligence. Thus also the value of commonly acknowledged principles and rules of interpretation as means to guide the interpreter; for the more the latter bases his judgment upon the traditional meanings rooted in the common experience of those who came before him, the more his mind is likely to become a steady focus for the expression of universal intelligence - a focus unblurred by individual biases or argumentative attitudes of the intellect.

In horary astrology the individual faces the universal; the part faces the whole. Horary astrology works because the whole acts upon the part whenever that part is in vital need. Just as the human body as a whole secretes instantly anti-toxins and hormones to come to the help of any injured cell or organ, so God (as personification of universal intelligence and spiritual vitality) always seeks to restore harmony and health in every individual whom life has thrown off balance. This divine effort to re-establish harmony in every disturbed individual is the substance of "Grace". It is the Whole coming to the help of every one of its parts. Horary astrology is a dramatic presentation of the operation of this divine Grace. Every *properly timed* horary chart is a celestial pantomime through which the universe seeks to impress a message upon every man in a state of crisis or vital difficulty.

It must be "properly timed", and horary astrology offers technical means to show whether or not the question has been asked at a significant time. These are the traditional "considerations before judgment" and even more perhaps the state of correlation between the horary chart and the natal chart of an enquirer. A horary chart is "radical" if it shows itself to be in close structural relationship to the situation it is called upon to resolve into harmony. Here also the fact that an astrologer is asked to cast a horary chart helps greatly to establish a proper timing. The chart is properly erected for the time when the impartial mediator (the astrologer) becomes aware of the situation - when he is asked the question. He is to provide the focus of the interpretation, the channelling of universal intelligence into humanly understandable words and directives. It is thus as his attention is at first focused upon the matter that the "act of Grace" is released which can solve the problem.

The real function of horary astrology is to establish a state of relationship between universal intelligence or divine Grace and the individual person buffetted by the cyclic storms or repolarization and the baffling confrontations of experience. It is not "fortune telling" as an escape from personal responsibility and effort, still less for curiosity's sake. It is instead a sign of the conscious binding of the individual to the rhythm and purpose of the universal Whole in which he accepts full and deliberate participation. From this Whole the individual receives understanding and healing, and the key to his many problems, *in proportion as* he is willing to consciously fulfill his function and his destiny.

THE THIRTEENTH STEP

The Establishment of Larger Frames of Reference for Individual Charts

No individual exists in a vacuum. He is related to other individuals, to groups of various kinds, to vast collectivities of men organized into societies, nations, cultural and religious denominations. He is one at root with mankind. He is an atom of consciousness within the vast ocean of intelligence, of which the multitudinous host of stars are the light-radiating spray, as this ocean breaks upon the shores of our space-time world. How could the destiny of the individual be separated from the vast web of universal destinies? How could the fleeting moment of his first salute to the universe - his birth-cry - remain isolated from the cycles of ever-flowing, ever-changing universal time? As every force and every mass interacts with every other force and every other mass, so the individuality of a man interacts with all other individual units of consciousness. There can be no separation, even where there is temporary isolation. We may look at the colored shapes of the tapestry of Being and admire the little curling loops of threads which make these shapes; but narrow indeed is our understanding if we fail to realize that these threads are long units weaving in and out, held together by the warp and woof of the universe.

The philosophically minded astrologer has always recognized these truths, and many have thought in various ways to discover methods by means of which they might be brought to a concrete focus of expression in astrological practice. Today some degree of attention is given to the comparison of the charts of people who belong to the same family or who are seeking to unite their lives for private or public purposes. "Astrological heredity" has been studied in an attempt to show the significant way in which the birth-charts of children, parents and more remote ancestors fall into correlated patterns, and the field such inquiries open is vast and as yet barely explored. It may be possible in this manner to isolate special emphases which, astrologically speaking, may serve to define the typical characteristics of a family - especially such family as retains a striking historical individuality through several generations of significant personalities. A study of great aristocratic, religious and royal ancestral lines of families in which outstanding cultural traits are retained for a time (as, for instance, the Bach family) would undoubtedly reveal most significant material. One wonders if Chinese astrologers have done such a work in relation to the family of Confucius, the direct line descendant of whom is living today after more than seventy generations.

Another and related field of study deals with the correlations between the birth-charts of men who have become partners, or who have succeeded one another in some great public enterprise. There have been statistical analyses of the charts of the Signers of the Declaration of Independence, and of the American Presidents; and a few significant points have emerged. More familiar to the astrological student and of more practical value is, however, the comparison between the birth-charts of prospective marriage partners, or even business partners. Every astrologer has been asked by friends and clients to find out if such and such person would make a "good partner", and the question is legitimately answerable *provided* a number of factors are taken into consideration. A horary chart and if possible a study of the celestial pattern on the day of the first meeting (or the first *significant and personalized* contact) are also of great value when such questions have to be answered; and they should be asked and answered in the spirit of the discussion concerning horary astrology in the preceding chapter.

The factors to be taken into consideration whenever the matter of a prospective marriage or partnership is brought forth can be stated in the form of a question to the enquirer: What do you consider to be the purpose of your relationship? It is at times a difficult question to answer, especially where love and marriage are concerned. But the answer of itself is often very revealing. It is always a *necessary factor* in the astrological judgment, if it is an honest answer.

If a conventional and smooth type of happiness is the purpose of the enquirer, a certain kind of planetary interrelationship between the two charts could be taken as a sign that the purpose is within reach, provided the partners' natal charts in themselves, and also progressions, transits and horary indications concur. But there may be cases in which the enquirer is seeking for a union of a more stirring and creative - or regenerative - character. He or she may say so deliberately; or it may become evident to the astrologer, in one way or another, that underneath a more conventional statement or aim, such a purpose is the deeper reality of the situation. Then a different type of astrological relationship should be looked for between the two charts, one which does not bar conflict, crisis and opposition between complementary viewpoints. Smoothness of personal relationship may mean a spiritual falling asleep, and if the individual seeks to become ever more fully awake as a creative soul and mind, should he or she not be warned of the possible results of a relationship in which elements *unfavorable to his or her purpose,* though favorable to the more banal type of union, are in evidence?

This point is made here only in order to show and to stress that astrology, if it is to be used significantly and spiritually, must always include the factor of *individual purpose* - and as well of individual function within a larger whole. A birth-chart is essentially a statement of purpose - God's purpose, one might say, in producing the conditions of birth and a soul to meet them. It is thus also a statement of what the individual's aim in life *should* be, if true to the creative Idea in the universal Mind. In the case of the horary chart, the chart is a statement of the solution symbolically expressed by the universal Intelligence in answer to the vital need of an individual and in terms of his essential purpose.

When the astrologer seeks to advise his client in the matter of a partnership or association on the basis of a comparison between birth-charts, he should thus be extremely careful to consider first of all what the purpose of the client's individual destiny is - therefore, the client's birth-chart. He should ascertain also how far the client understands this basic purpose, and what his conscious aim is in the particular instance under consideration. To give astrological advice does not mean merely to look at one or more charts and to state blandly and without concern what one sees, rightly or wrongly. It means to help the client to understand how he can best reach *his true purpose of destiny.* And the way to such a purpose is not always the way of conventional happiness!

Thus far I have considered mainly the relationship of individuals to individuals in partnership or limited groups. But we should never forget that human beings are not born as individuals; that the status of individual selfhood is reached by human beings only after a very long process of historical evolution. First, came the tribal group - a biologically rooted organism of unconscious human beings kept integrated by the compulsive power of *tabus* and of the law of a deified Great Ancestor. Gradually tribes evolved into kingdoms ruled by kings and priests, expanding through conquest and becoming increasingly heterogeneous because of blood-mixture. As a result of social and racial, economic and religious conflicts, the types of society and of states found in the pre-Christian era developed about the time our Western kind of astrology reached its traditional form in Chaldea and later in Greece and Alexandria.

Archaic astrology did not deal with individuals, simply because no human being at the time was actually considered to be an individual, except the king or high-priest - and this only in a symbolical, rather impersonal (or super-personal) way. Astrology then had a strictly collective purpose. It sought to establish an ordered foundation for all social and agricultural activity on the basis of the order displayed by the heavens. Astrology was entirely "mundane"; that is, it dealt with affairs of state, weather and agriculture, with the outcome of wars and the destinies of empires. As the king and the kingdom were entirely identified with each other, charts erected for the accession of the king to the throne were considered as valid expressions of the nature and destiny of the kingdom during that particular reign. The emphasis, however, was not placed on the king as an individual, but upon the "office". The king (or high-priest or any holder of office) was not considered as an individual man, but as the incorporation of a collective tribal or state function. The function was important, not the person fulfilling it. If marriage between two persons was decided upon by a study of their birth-charts, the matter was, for many centuries, one to be solved primarily with regard to the biological and social-economic productivity of the prospective couple. Marriage, too, was regarded exclusively as a social function; not as a partnership between individuals.

All astrology dealt therefore with collective "offices" and "functions", or with the anticipation of natural events (inundations, storms, droughts, etc.) Birth-charts were not erected as indicators of the destiny and character of individuals, considered strictly as isolated individual entities, until the Greco-Latin period - especially in Rome and Alexandria. From then on, astrology was divided into two basically distinct fields: *natal* and *mundane,* the former dealing with "individual souls"; the latter, with "collective destiny", state offices and natural phenomena. Because the last ten or more centuries have been characterized (especially in the Western world) by an extreme of confusion concerning the relationship between collective and individual factors, these two branches of astrology have not been clearly enough differentiated. "Natal" and "mundane" techniques have been mixed, and the new factors in human society have not been given their due recognition in adequate astrological procedures.

The last decades, however, have witnessed interesting and probably very significant attempts to regenerate mundane astrology and to discover techniques which would fit the entirely new conditions in which groups and nations act and interact in the modern world. Among the most widely known I shall mention:

1. *The erection of corporate "birth-charts"*. Since Roman Law recognized the fact that business organizations or similar types of groups are entitled to the legal status of "personality", the field has been open for considering nations as vast collective persons with individualized characters, such as culture, language, general temperament, destiny and collective purpose. As collective persons, nations could be given "birth-charts", national planetary rulers and all that belongs to the field of natal astrology - in the same way in which a corporation is given a birth-chart erected for the time of incorporation. However, such a corporate national birth-chart can be said to exist *only* when some kind of Covenant, or specific collective Act, can be referred to: election, signing of document, proclamation, or the like.

In such a case, whoever is born as part of the nation thus "incorporated" participates in the *collective national purpose*, whether or not he is aware of the fact. This participation becomes an integral part of his own individual purpose, and must be recognized as such. This was not true in ancient societies in which a state was the creation of a king, expanded by the king's marriage, etc. There was a "state" but no "nation" - and no corporate national birth-chart, only *the chart of a "reign"*, or at best of an "ancestral tradition" dominating all the subjects of the kingdom with the power of an instinctual root-compulsion; and the difference between root-compulsion and participation in a corporate purpose is very great indeed!

2. *Geographical areas and zodiacal rulership.* In Ptolemaic astrology "zodiacal rulerships" were attributed to rather vaguely defined regions of the then known world - each broad region being correlated to a sign of the zodiac. The zones of rulership radiated in a somewhat peculiar manner from the Mediterrean sea, center of the civilization of the period. In the course of centuries, these zones became the dwelling places of numerous nations; so that rather dissimilar nations still retained the same zodiacal sign as

ruler (for instance, France and Italy, under Leo; England, Denmark and Germany under Aries, etc.) The validity of these rulerships has been challenged and modified by astrologers; new rulerships have been attributed to cities, provinces, etc. This has led to much confusion.

Several decades ago Albert Ross Parsons (and later Sepharial) sought to establish a direct correlation between bands of earth-longitude and zodiacal signs or constellations, on the principle that the earth globe could be considered as a microcosm of the macrocosm, the celestial sphere. Granted that such a correspondence between the celestial sphere and our globe is possible, two problems must be solved: A. Does the correspondence refer to *constellations,* or to *signs* of the zodiac? B. From where do we have to start - that is, what longitude on earth corresponds to Aries 0°?

According to Parsons each geographical continent and region corresponds to, and has affinity for, one particular constellation of fixed stars - always the same. This type of correspondence might be said to be the same as that according to which Aries "rules" the head, Taurus the neck, Gemini the shoulders and lungs, etc. Man is seen as the microcosm and the universe as the macrocosm - and the correspondence between the two has proven its worth beyond doubt in *natal* astrology. Symbolical diagrams have been made in which a man bent backward, with feet touching head, is encircled by the zodiac, Aries at the head, Pisces at the feet.

In such a symbolical correlation, however, what should be made to correspond to the human body, I believe, is *not* the zodiac of constellations, but the zodiac of signs. In other words, it is the first month after the vernal equinox - i.e. the beginning of spring - which corresponds to the head, not a group of fixed stars; and the feet are connected with the last of the twelve divisions of the solar year rather than with the constellation Pisces. This same type of equivalence could be used, substituting the earth's globe for the human body. However, the difficulty then is of deciding which longitudinal section of the earth's surface corresponds to the *sign*

Aries - and by implication to the human head. It has been assumed, in England especially, that the Greenwich meridian corresponds to Aries 0°; but such an assumption can certainly be challenged. The problem refers to what we might call "occult geography" and the field is too big, its implications too far reaching, to be discussed here.

The type of correspondence which Albert Ross Parsons was interested in was, however, one in which the entire celestial map of the constellations could be focused upon the entire globe of the earth and particular stars would be connected with particular geographical locations. But, from this point of view, it is fairly evident that one should take into consideration the fact that the zodiacal longitudes of stars change constantly, due to the cyclic movement called "precession of the equinoxes". If the celestial sphere is projected upon our globe, the equator and the ecliptic are two circles which intersect each other; and their points of intersection (Aries and Libra 0°) shift constantly westward, accomplishing a complete circuit in about 25,868 years. This shift can be related to the often mentioned "westward march of empires". It can be taken to mean that a projection of the star-patterns (constellations) upon our globe should likewise shift. Thus the constellation which could be said to "rule" England in the year 1000 A.D. is now ruling the vast expanse of the Atlantic Ocean. It will rule once more what remains of the British Isles around 27,000 A.D.

It is upon such a type of reasoning that Edward Johndro established about twenty years ago his system of geographical astrology, and sought to help individuals to discover the location to which their own birth-charts attuned them most favorable. Another astrologer, Paul Councel, worked along similar lines, but on a different basis, giving to the phenomenon of precession of the equinoxes an interpretation which differs fundamentally from the one accepted by modern astronomers. The practical problem is, in either case, how to determine the geographical longitude on which the spring equinox or vernal Sun is to be projected at any specified time. Johndro placed Aries 0° today at about 30° longitude West. Councel says that the vernal equinox was in 1932 at longitude 35°50' West (cf. "Cosmic Causation in Geophysics", 1945). Both calculations seem to me not to conform exactly enough with the actual historical events recording the westward sweep of the main focus, or foci, of human civilization during the last millennia - unless of course one gives to our European civilization a somewhat peculiar meaning. Here again everything depends upon one's interpretation; and provided one does not seek too obviously to make history fit a preconceived pattern, the historical validity and significance of the parallelism is presumably the only criterion we have in determining which longitudinal belt corresponds to which zodiacal sign or constellation.

The matter cannot be discussed further here. All that I wanted to show was that, if such a theory of shifting zodiacal rulership for regions of earth longitude is correct, a man born anywhere on the globe would also find himself related to a constellation and a star by virtue of his birthplace. But as these geo-celestial relationships are shifting according to the 25,868 year cycles of civilization, what this actually means is that a man's life can be seen *as occupying a definite place (thus function) in this vast precessional cycle*. This is his largest "frame of reference" and his exact place in it can be determined *by the longitude of his birth-place at the time of his birth*. If this is understood, it can also be admitted that a man can modify his place and function in this "frame of reference" *by changing his residence* - which opens a very interesting field of investigation, provided one understands what is really at stake.

Moreover the place and function of an individual in the large "frame of reference" of the 25,868 year cycle can be measured, not only by the *place* of his birth, but also by the *generation* to which he belongs. If one could be certain of the time when the precessional cycle began (a matter unfortunately not yet settled either!), each generation could be said to belong to a particular fraction (zodiacal degree) of this precessional cycle. For instance, if the vernal equinox is today (and approximately since 1916) located within the second degree of Pisces (which means that the Aquarian Age would begin next century) then every person born, let us say between 1844 and 1916 would "belong" to the third degree of Pisces. This degree would set his collective, over-all "human" significance in terms of the development of civilization and of mankind in general - in so far as *time-values* are concerned. Then if he were born at a place "ruled" by, say, the first degree of the constellation Taurus, this fact would establish the nature of his participation in the larger cycle, as far as *space-values* are concerned.

To the average person, concerned almost exclusively with his ego and his family, such a type of larger frame of reference can have but little meaning. He may be caught in a crises of civilization, such as our World-Wars; but he is swept by collective forces, of which he has no consciousness and over which he has no control. It is only the individual who is a public leader, in one field or another, who can be said to deal *consciously* with such larger issues affecting nations and civilizations.

The astrological relationship of such a man with vast collective issues is two-fold: on the one hand, his birth-chart can be compared with the corporate chart of the group or nation in which he actively participates - and this shows the relationship between his individual life-purpose and the basic purpose of his collectivity. On the other hand, both the time and the place of his birth establish his two-fold *subservience* to the type of all-human, planetary (or "divine") forces which are affecting the general processes of civilization in so far as his generation and his country of birth (and, secondarily, of residence) are concerned. Unfortunately, the exact character of this subservience can only be determined astrologically when astrologers succeed in firmly establishing the exact starting points, in time and space, of this 25,868 year cycle of precession of the equinoxes.

Mundane astrology, properly speaking, does not deal with individuals as such, but only with the relationships they have with

large-scale collective issues. Too much attention, I believe, is placed
upon the charts of Presidents or Prime Ministers in seeking to
forecast trends in the nations whose destinies they seem to control
for a while. What matters, rather, is the *relationship* between the
leaders and their nation's charts - or the charts of their assumption
of office. Mundane astrology, at the level of *conscious action by
conscious individuals,* is a matter of inter-relationship between
charts - thus, its extreme complexity today. And at the level of
unconscious subservience to the rhythm of the march of civilization, mundane astrology refers to cycles which constitute still uncertain frames of reference - thus, its lack of accuracy.

Mundane astrologers, in ancient times, laid great stress upon
the cycle of conjunction of Jupiter and Saturn (at 20-year intervals) and upon eclipse cycles. Today Jupiter and Saturn are but
secondary indicators of social changes in a world in which tribal
and national boundaries no longer contain the tides of human interchanges; and their cycles are being superseded, in all world-wide
issues, by those of Uranus, Neptune and Pluto, which subdivide
approximate 500 and 1000 year cycles - the basic measures. Yet
the death in office of American Presidents elected under a Jupiter-Saturn conjunction reminds us of the validity of such a cycle.
Thanks to the work of Charles E. Jayne, eclipse cycles have also
been given a new meaning in terms of a study of the geographical paths traced on our globe by the shadow of total eclipse. Larger cycles are thus coming to light.

The fact that now human beings are beginning to leave, for increasingly long periods of time, the surface of our globe and even
the gravitational field of the earth is posing new theoretical problems to the astrologer. We may have to devise in the future a
new kind of "solar system astrology"; and I have discussed at
various times (cf. WORLD ASTROLOGY - 1944 -1945) what I
consider to be a more sound approach to "heliocentric" astrology.
The advocates of a "sidereal zodiac of constellations" which they
claim should supersede the "tropical zodiac of signs" may also be
paving the way for a significant study of the relationship of the

earth to the galaxy as a whole. Our sun is but a minor star in this vast array of celestial bodies, the galaxy, which most likely is the most characteristic unit of cosmic organization; and the cycle established by the revolution of this sun around the core of the galaxy - about 400 millions of years - should some day be considered. Even today the discoveries of Professor Piccardi suggest that the ever-changing angle formed by the plane of the earth's equator and the basic plane of the lens-shaped galaxy is related to slight but significant changes in the operations of living organisms; this through the intermediary of the water contained in the body, for water seems to be most sensitive to an as-yet unknown galactic force.

Vast perspectives are indeed opening up to the human mind. Will our official science, fascinated by technological problems and refusing to accept any concept which does not fit in with the method of a rigorous and strictly intellectual approach to thinking, prove to be able always to satisfy man's restless search for universal meaning? I, for one, doubt it. Other approaches will have to be devised, incorporating the strictly scientific methods, but also accepting the guidance of and the data provided by other than merely intellectual faculties.

The place astrology will have in the new global cilivization which we see emerging before our eyes can hardly be predicted. If it is to have a significant place, it should abandon the present-day popular aspect which commercial interests appealing to the insecurity and restlessness of modern men and women have unfortunately (but inevitably) featured. In any case we should never forget that astrology did represent the primordial search of human beings for measurable order and basic meaning in their collective and individual existence; and the search is never ended.

This search is quite distinct from the urge to control our environment by technological means in order to provide maximum convenience and physical comfort to the largest possible number of human beings. The future of astrology does not rest, I believe, with its becoming some sort of statistically validated science; it depends rather on its capacity to balance and complement scientific, technological thinking by upholding a holistic search for ever more universalistic patterns of order revealing an ever deeper and inclusive realization of the meaning and rhythm of existence in an ever-widening world of human experience.

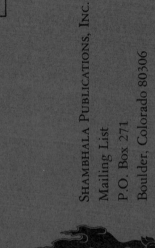

Shambhala Publications, Inc.
Mailing List
P.O. Box 271
Boulder, Colorado 80306

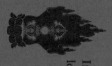

If you wish to receive a copy of the latest Shambhala Publications catalogue of books and to be placed on our mailing list please send us this card.

PLEASE PRINT

Book in which this card was found _____

Name: _____

Address: _____

City & State: _____

Zip or Postal Code: _____ Country (if outside U.S.A.): _____